Watch out for the rats!

Edvard. del R.

The King Rat

and His Court

Lessons in Corporate Greed

William Arthur Bruno
Illustrated by Eduardo del Río

For permission to reuse text copyrighted content from *The King Rat and His Court*, please got to www.copyright.com, or contact Copyright Clearance Center, 222 Rosewood Drive, Danvers, MA 01923, telephone 978-750-8400, fax 978-646-8600. Copyright Clearance Center is a not-for-profit organization that provides copyright licensing on behalf of William Arthur Bruno.

For permission to reuse illustration copyrighted content from *The King Rat and His Court*, please go to www.pencilprone.com for copyright licensing from Eduardo del Rio.

Publisher's Cataloging-in Publication Data

Bruno, William Arthur.

The king rat and his court: lessons in corporate greed / William Arthur Bruno ; illustrated by Eduardo del Rio

p.cm.

ISBN 1-4392-2192-8

1. Business ethics. 2. Corporations- Moral and ethical aspects. 3. Executives - Professional ethics.

HF5387 B78 2009
174'.4-dc22   2008911565

Designed by Eduardo del Rio

FIRST EDITION

ISBN-13: 978-1439221921

Published by BookSurge Publishing

Visit www.booksurge.com to order additional copies

Printed in the United States of America

For all those capable, ethical employees and retirees

who have suffered the loss of

jobs,

promotions,

pensions,

healthcare,

community services,

and financial wealth

due to the insatiable greed of

King Rats

CONTENTS

REFACE

The financial crisis that began in late 2008 has focused attention on political and corporate leadership in America. Our leaders have jeopardized the financial well-being of all Americans. Why have elected officials and corporate executives allowed the financial crisis to grow to such epic proportions? Why does there seem to be a lack of true leadership in government and in the boardroom? The answers given by the media do not seem credible to the public. There must be a systemic problem that lurks below the surface and operates in darkness.

Throughout my business career, I observed how truly difficult it is for outsiders to understand what goes on within a major organization. I have been stupefied by the tolerance for mediocre "leaders" who achieve positions of power in government and the corporate world. I have witnessed massive transfers of wealth and inherent economic inefficiencies that result from poor, corrupt leadership.

Why is there no backlash for the incompetent and fraudulent actions of such leaders, and why are unsavory behaviors allowed to perpetuate? Why don't free markets and open competition, coupled with the checks and balances of fiduciary boards of directors and government regulators, limit these behaviors? Why do these individuals seem to have immunity from laws and regulations, and from criticism by the media and academia? Finally, what has happened to the character, substance, wisdom and grace of those gaining wealth and power in our society?

The state of political and corporate governance is rewarding individuals who by their very nature are parasitic. Governance of our institutions has been taken over by those with insatiable appetites to amass wealth and power.

As I observed wayward leaders, what began to emerge in my mind was the similarity of their behavior to that of rats. I became proficient in anticipating their actions and explaining the reasons for their decisions by asking myself one simple question: What would a rat do if faced with such circumstances?

Many of you are undoubtedly familiar with Dr. Spencer Johnson's bestseller, written a decade ago, *Who Moved My Cheese?* (1998). Johnson uses cheese as a metaphor for all that you want in life, such as wealth, happiness, security, good health, and a nice home.

I believe that many corporate and political leaders have misused the message in books such as *Who Moved my Cheese?* Wayward leaders want you to believe that your misfortune is self-inflicted because of your failure to change; whereas, in many instances the real truth is that your misfortune is due to their poor leadership.

Dr. Johnson's book features two enterprising, little mice named "Sniff" and "Scurry". Ironic, is it not, that his positive role models for you are two rodents? Perhaps this is why so many corporate leaders have been attracted to the book – they share genetic code with those cute little mice!

There is no question that your cheese is gone or has been severely reduced. However, chances are your cheese hasn't been moved--rather, it has been stolen by rats:

• As a long-term, reliable employee, you have lost your job.
• As a union member, your contract is meaningless, your wages slashed, your pension and healthcare plans decimated, and your safety conditions in the workplace have deteriorated.
• As a surviving employee, your workload has multiplied with no prospect of promotion or reward.

- As a retiree, your healthcare benefits are reduced or eliminated, your pension is at risk, and your savings have diminished in value.
- As a shareholder, your equity has eroded.
- As a vendor, you are unable to secure contracts at competitive prices.
- As a community member, your local economy is in decline.

When patients present symptoms of drug overdose in the emergency room of a hospital, they are administered what is called a reversal agent. The reversal agent counteracts the physiological effects of the drug. This book is intended as a reversal agent for books written (or misused) by corporate rats. The "drugs" that we have ingested are propaganda pieces written to perpetuate the theft of your cheese, and to enrich the purveyors and their friends.

By the end of this book you will be able to identify those who have devoured your "cheese" and taken away your livelihood. You will know how it was taken. You will become an expert in identifying patterns of behavior. You will be able to test the organizations with which you are most familiar to determine their degree of infestation.

For those who would say that I am painting political and corporate leaders with too broad a brush, let me say that it is simply a matter of degree. The two questions you should ask are: (1) what is the degree of rat infestation in my organizations, and (2) what is the degree of deviance of my leaders? The answer on both counts is probably much more than you have been led to believe.

For those who would say that this will damage the respect that we have for people in positions of leadership, I would say good. Many do not deserve our respect. We should show respect for the position held by the leader, but not necessarily for the individual in that position. Respect is earned, it is not an entitlement. As in the military, salute "the bars on the shoulders", but not necessarily the person inside the uniform.

For those in leadership positions who do not exhibit rat-like behavior, you are to be commended. You have achieved your position despite significant handicap. You have succeeded with the odds stacked against you. You are the type of leader who should be promoted to positions of high responsibility; however, the incumbent rats will work overtime to make sure that does not happen.

Rats have existed throughout recorded history, and have been responsible for destruction and plagues. They exist in a parasitic relationship with their hosts for as long as they are controlled within limits. When infestation becomes problematic for the host, then the call for the exterminator resonates until the rat population is brought under control. The exterminator limits the number of rats to a tolerable level for the host. Then, once complacency again besets the host, the cycle reverses and the rat population resumes its growth. It is no coincidence that the corporate community cycles through a crisis every decade. The rats need to be brought under control to prevent killing the host.

I have written this book to shed daylight on the behavior of corporate rats--something these nocturnal creatures disdain. In doing so, it is necessary to study their ethology in the quest for wealth and power. The term "ethology" was coined in 1843 in John Stuart Mill's *A System of Logic* (1874). Ethology, according to Mill, is "the science of the formation of character" (Ibid.,596). This science "determines the kind of character produced in conformity to those general laws of psychology, by any set of circumstances, physical and moral" (Ibid.,602). Mill applied what is called the Lamarckian view of the development of character--that "the rational choices of one generation predispose the tastes of subsequent generations to reinforce similar choices."(Persky 1995,226). In the 20th century, ethology has become known as the scientific study of animal behavior (Barnett 1963). Human ethology is more commonly known today as the field of sociobiology.

Rats at birth and through demonstrators develop an amazing adherence to the feeding habits and lifestyle of their predecessors (Bekoff 2004). Mill believed that parsimony exercised by leaders was essential for the success of our economic system (Persky 1995). Rats do not display parsimonious behavior; nor do many of our leaders.

By exposing the King Rat and studying his ethology, my hope is that we can reduce the infestation in our institutions and prevent the plague from spreading. Those are ambitious goals. In the interim, I hope that you gain personal respect for how you have conducted yourself. Our free-market economy depends on hard work, enterprising individuals, and a high level of ethics for sustainability.

You are the reason for the success of our economic system, and you deserve better than you have received. Taking action to reform our leadership is the responsibility of all, and collectively we can win back our economic and political systems from the rats.

One final note. All characters in The King Rat and His Court are fictitious. Any resemblance of these rodent characters to any persons living or dead is purely coincidental.

Let's get on with exposing the rats to daylight!

William Arthur Bruno
Pittsburgh, Pennsylvania
February 2009

SECTION I

The Inner Court

Make an incision through the skin only in the mid-ventral line of the abdomen and cut toward the mouth and then to the posterior to the ventral sides of the legs, avoiding the external genitalia. Using the fingers, tear the skin away from the underlying body wall and deflect to the sides, taking care in the regions of the armpits, neck and groin where blood vessels are close to the surface.

How to Skin a Rat
The Rat: A Practical Guide, **1964**

King Rat and the members of his Inner Court have remarkable similarities to the Urban Brown Rat species (*Rattus norvegicus*). Brown Rats, the largest of the 56 species in the genus *Rattus*, are the vermin most familiar to city dwellers (Morris and Beer 2003). They prefer living on the ground and are excellent diggers. They create extensive burrow systems with many entrances and chambers for escape paths, security, and feeding. Brown Rats are suspicious animals making them very difficult to catch alive or even to photograph (Boot 1985). They will eat anything, but especially enjoy meat. Contrary to popular thought, cheese is not their favorite delicacy. But we will continue with this folklore, since cheese is more palatable than rotten fish or decaying chicken--two favorites of the Urban Brown Rat (Henrickson 1983).

Philosophers and theologians over the millennia have provided an understanding of man's quest to achieve power and wealth by analogy to rat-like behavior. Without native intelligence, physical strength or self-confidence, such behavior enables an individual to overcome his innate shortcomings. If you can't win by playing fair, why play fair? As the prizes from feeding and breeding become larger, the rewards outweigh the risks of being a rat. The weak or mediocre can tilt the playing field. Better yet, a person with gifts of high intelligence and business acumen can overtake others possessing similar gifts, but who do not exhibit the behavior of a rat. Just like performance enhancing drugs, rat-like behavior gives that extra boost to make it into the corner office.

Let's skin the King Rat and his Court to expose their inner workings and explain their actions. The chief executive officer and his six closest associates make up the Inner Court. Ten organizations make up the Outer Court, sustaining the King Rat. Several members of the Outer Court have multiple constituents. Therefore, the Outer Court may involve 20 to 30 principal players. There may be many more bit players, in the range of 100 to 200, depending on the proclivities of the King Rat. However, those in this latter category are facilitators, rather then hard core members of the King's Court.

Rat packs in the urban environment are said to range in size from 15 to 220 rats, based on observations by rodentologists (ibid.). It is no surprise that the King Rat and his Court mimic these numbers.

Before dissecting a rat, you need to carefully skin the rat so that you can expose its internal parts. While making the incision, your self-control with the scalpel may be tested. An inadvertent slip of the scalpel has been known to happen, particularly in the posterior near the ventral side of the legs of male rats.

CHAPTER 1
Chief Executive Officer—"The King Rat"

And the strongest was always the King, not by strength alone, but King by cunning and luck and strength together. Among the rats.

King Rat
James Clavell, 1962

The chief executive officer is the King Rat, or simply King. King is the ultimate goal for a corporate rat. How does a rat get to be named CEO in the first place? You will learn the tricks when we discuss the board of directors and the outsiders who serve the King. But let's put it this way: King has a proven record as a rat in other organizations. He has distributed so much cheese to friends in positions of authority, that when an opening appears, all those fed by him in the past will throw lavish praise his way.

A King Rat almost always comes from outside the organization. He has been brought in as an agent of change, even if no change is needed. If there is no change, then the members of the Outer Court are not fed, and the King loses his power.

In most cases, King is not the brightest candle. However, he is cunning and devious. With a long history of stealing from others, he has refined his talent. He knows how to steal the maximum amount of cheese without getting caught.

The King rarely appears to the minions in the company. However, you know what he looks like since his picture is plastered all over company newsletters, annual reports and media appearances to take credit for any successes. If you are an employee of a company headed by a King Rat, you are meaningless to him. You cannot do anything for the King, except perhaps interfere with his feeding. King needs to spend all of his time with outside rats that can feed him in ways far exceeding his reported compensation.

The only goals of the King Rat are to feed and breed--to maximize his wealth at the expense of shareholders, employees, retirees and communities in which the company operates. He is not interested in running the company, or exposing himself to accountability. Hard work and accountability are for losers.

To ensure that he is not accountable for anything, King Rat organizes his management to distance himself from engineering, operations and sales. The incumbents in these critical line positions are not part of   the King's Court. King inserts   expendable   intermediaries into his chain of command. If   revenues are down for whatever reason, he   blames the head of sales. If product is   late or defective, he   blames   the head of engineering. If quality is poor, costs are high, or worker safety is deteriorating, he blames the operators. The more times King Rat fires an intermediary and reorganizes the business, the better Wall Street likes him. Likewise, the more searches that are done to replace those fired, the more cheese goes to the executive search firm building loyalty to the King.

With no real responsibility, King just needs to show up at meetings with his Court to give directions on how he wants them to steal your cheese. The meetings may be held at the local country club so that King can sup in style at company expense. King never pays for anything out of his own pocket.

A King Rat must protect himself from any accountability or exposure. He lays down so much insulation you would think the Pink Panther is one of his preferred suppliers. His insulation is the Inner Court. To form his court he finds ways to replace the incumbent executive staff members with those that he can own as vassals. If you happen to be the incumbent in one of these positions--too bad.

He sniffs out individuals from both within the organization and known outsiders who will meet his needs. Those brought in from the outside are acquaintances of the King, and they already have proven their lack of ethical standards. Others may be elevated from inside the company if they display depravity pleasing to the King. King is the demonstrator rat. Younger rats smell food on the demonstrator and want it--even if it will harm them (Dugatkin 2000).

The candidates for membership to the Inner Court fall into two distinct categories. The first category consists of members who have potential to become future King Rats after serving as apprentices in the Court. The second category includes individuals who have no potential or desire whatsoever to advance to CEO positions. Those in the latter category are preferred for most positions, as they are non-threatening. The King shares your cheese with them, so that they become dependent on him for a lifestyle beyond their wildest dreams.

The royal household of a 12th Century monarch included a hierarchy of officers and royal clerks, a steward, chief huntsman, hawker and groom, chamber servants and household troops (Cannon and Griffiths 1988). The names may have changed, but the royal court of the King Rat serves many of the same functions.

Let's examine the signs that suggest your CEO is truly of the species *Rattus*:

• Employees outside of the Inner Court rarely see the King unless the event is highly programmed in advance by a member of the Court.

• The King and his Court have a private parking area, a separate entrance, and an office located in an executive wing or floor, so as to avoid detection of coming and going, and to avoid contact with the employees.

• Members of his Court have grand offices that surround the King, rather than being located in the departments they oversee.

• The King has a private jet for business trips and pleasure trips which are disguised as business trips. The board establishes policies that gross-up compensation to cover reported personal trips so that he is not affected by additional taxes. Professor David Yermack (2005a) at NYU's Stern School of Business found that average shareholder returns underperformed market benchmarks by more than four percent annually when firms disclosed the perk of personal use of corporate aircraft. Abuse of corporate jet usage is common. King Rat uses the jet to transport his children to summer camp, for European family vacations, trips to NCAA basketball tournaments, or to pick up household

Amid Crackdown, the Jet Perk Suddenly Looks a Lot Pricier

Companies have long defended corporate jets as vital business tools, needed to efficiently convey top executives to far-flung operations or meetings. But new disclosures, prompted in large part by a crackdown by the Securities and Exchange Commission, show that executives are using jets for vacation and leisure travel to a far greater extent than previously known.

The SEC crackdown, which came after officials were convinced that many companies were hiding or undercounting the cost of this sensitive perk, has led to many more companies revealing six-figure spending on their executive's personal jet travel. At least 33 executives received more than $200,000 apiece in personal-plane benefits in 2004, a Wall Street Journal analysis of recent proxy filings shows. In a few cases, frequent-flier executives are reaping more in personal trips aboard the corporate plane than in salary. Meanwhile, executives must report only a tiny fraction of these costs as income under separate Internal Revenue Service rules – and some companies grant them extra pay to cover the resulting taxes.

....

Many...companies cite security concerns in explaining use of the personal jet. Some require their top executives to use the corporate craft for personal as well as business travel. Until recently, the more aggressive of these companies took the stance that the security policies meant personal flying wasn't a perk that needed to be disclosed.

items. Some King Rats ring up hundreds of thousands of dollars annually in personal use of corporate aircraft, and, analysts believe that the amounts reported may be understated by a factor of two to three times (Maremont 2005).

- The King announces expense account policies that are draconian to the employees. These rules apply only to non-Court members, while he spares no expense on himself and his Court:
  - He arranges hunting trips with members of his Court and tries to find a customer or supplier to take along to justify the business purpose.
  - He buys season tickets for the local professional teams so that his Court can take their families to games. Rarely do customers or the other employees see the tickets.
  - He belongs to several country clubs at company expense, so he can entertain the Outside Court who will be feeding on your cheese. Personal use of corporate aircraft and long distance golf memberships show significant correlation (Yermack 2005a).
  - He makes sure the company has a project near his vacation home so that he can fly there on company expense. Better yet, he has been known to move the company headquarters to his hometown.
- The King spends most of his time meeting with outsiders, except when important inside business issues arise--such as his employment contract, golden parachute, increased board compensation, and directors' and officers' insurance.

When first brought into a sound company, the King Rat is the weakest level in management. Over time the weakness cascades progressively to lower levels as competent employees are replaced by the King or leave on their own accord when they view

....

Corporate watchdogs are skeptical of the security argument, except for a few high-profile CEOs. "These are the people most able to afford it themselves, so why are stockholders subsidizing their leisure time?" says Paul Hodgson of The Corporate Library, a corporate-governance advisory firm in Portland, Maine. "It seems to be wholly inappropriate."

Wall Street Journal May 25, 2005
Copyright © 2005 Dow Jones & Company Inc.

their situation as being hopeless. The average tenure of the King in a company depends on its strength when he first arrives. The stronger the company, the more cheese he has to steal--extending his longevity. A typical reign is about five years, at which time most of the cheese has been stolen, and the King moves to the next feeding ground.

The King Rat is taking advantage of the power of oligarchy. The "iron law of oligarchy" is attributed to Robert Michels in his 1915 classical work: *Political Parties: A Sociological Study of the Oligarchical Tendencies of Modern Democracy* (1966). Michels was a German-born Italian political sociologist. In Michels' theory of organization, large-scale organizations give their officers a near monopoly of power. This is an intrinsic part of bureaucracy. Says Michels, "It is organization which gives birth to the domination of the elected over the electors, of the mandataries over the mandators, of the delegates over the delegators. Who says organization, says oligarchy"(ibid.,365).

The CEOs in large organizations are given a near monopoly of power through superior access to knowledge, control of communications and skill at politics (ibid.). Their self-importance is totally a function of their command of an organization.

Although Michels wrote about political parties, the corporation has become a single-party, political organization. Michels warned his students to be aware whenever they sense that leadership is deviating from professional goals and rational systems. Whenever this occurs, the purpose of obtaining power is to exploit the masses to extend their own privilege and power rather than for the good of the organization.

Michels went on to describe the personal lust for power that is characteristic of leaders. He claimed that this intensifies their efforts to enhance their power, and that leaders revert to ulterior devices toward that end. They develop a vested interest in their positions that must be protected. Michels further recognized that with long tenure in office, leaders become firmly entrenched. "The masses in such cases are often sulky, but they never rebel, for they lack the power to punish the treachery of the chiefs" (ibid.,169). Nearly 100 years since his classic work on oligarchial tendencies, we see his fears of leaders abusing their power played out in the modern corporation.

In *The Economics of Innocent Fraud*, John Kenneth Galbraith (2004) observed that the passage of power in the corporation has moved from (originally) the owners, to (next) the stockholders, and (now) to the management.

Michels and Galbraith provide the underpinnings of why we list the chief executive officer first, and name him the King Rat. The board of directors and the stockholders are subordinate to the chief executive officer. The board of directors is clearly second, and

Mao and the Art of Management

The disparity between Mao's performance and his reputation is instructive, for behind it are four key ingredients which all bad managers could profitably employ.

A powerful, mendacious slogan

Born a modestly well-off villager, Mao lived like an emperor, carried on litters by peasants, surrounded by concubines and placated by everyone. Yet his most famous slogan was "Serve the People". This paradox illustrates one aspect of his brilliance: his ability to justify his actions, no matter how entirely self-serving, as being done for others.

Psychologists call this "cognitive dissonance" – the ability to make a compelling, heartfelt case for one thing while doing another. Being able to pull off this sort of trick is an essential skill in many professions. It allows sub-standard chief executives to rationalise huge pay packages while their underlings get peanuts (or rice).....

Ruthless media manipulation

....Chief executives are not in a position to crush the media as Mao did. Nevertheless, his handling of them offers some lessons. He talked only to sycophantic journalists and his appeal in the West came mainly from hagiographies written by reporters whose careers were built on the access they had to him.

Sacrifice of friends and colleagues

Mao...did not want people too close to him, and therefore

the owners--the stockholders--come last. The power is reverse from what is intended.

The CEO is self-rewarded as he sets his own compensation and orchestrates board meetings. The board is expected to be acquiescent to the CEO. This is a clear sign, according to Galbraith, that the economic world and the political world are becoming one. This power play cannot succeed without the complicity of the board--and most importantly without the chairman of the board.

As King Rats proliferate and more companies become infested, it becomes increasingly difficult to exterminate them. The playing field tilts in favor of the rats. As long as the growth of the rat population remains unchecked, plague will follow.

RAT PATROL

In the Appendix of this book, you will find a test to determine the **DRIAD** (pronounced "dry-add")--the **D**egree of **R**at **I**nfestation **A**nd **D**eviance of your organization and leadership. Detection is incredibly difficult. The King and His Court are nocturnal animals, and exhibit thigmotropic behavior (staying in close contact with walls to avoid being caught in the open). You know that rats are present by seeing evidence of their droppings to power; so being Mao's friend often proved more dangerous than being his enemy. One purge followed another...

Enemies, conversely can be useful. Mao often blamed battlefield losses on rivals who were made to suffer for these defeats. The names of modern victims of this tactic will be visible on the list of people sacked at an investment bank after a rough quarter; the practitioners are their superiors, or those who have taken their jobs.

Activity substituting for achievement

...Under Mao, China didn't drift, it careened. The propellant came from the top. Policies were poor, execution dreadful and leadership misdirected, but each initiative seemed to create a centripetal force, as everyone looked to Beijing to see how to march forward (or avoid being trampled). The business equivalent of this is restructuring, the broader the better. Perhaps for the struggling executive, this is the single most important lesson: if you can't do anything right, do a lot. The more you have going on, the longer it will take for its disastrous consequences to become clear. And think very big: for all his flaws, Mao was inspiring.

In the long run, of course, the facts will find you out. But who cares? We all know what we are in the long run.

Economist December 22, 2007
Copyright 2007 by Economist Newspaper Group

and their trail of destruction; however, you rarely, if ever, see them. At the conclusion of each chapter on the members of the Court, the Rat Patrol will present lessons for detecting corporate greed. By learning these lessons, you will be prepared to test the **DRIAD** of your organization.

The key to detecting a King Rat is intellectual curiosity. To borrow an overused word from the war on terrorism--you must be "vigilant." Curiosity and vigilance will uncover the truth about the King Rat. Political and corporate leaders depend upon the laziness and naiveté of their constituents. You will have to change your mindset and think like a rat to be able to hone in on illicit behavior. However... a word of caution...although you must think like a rat, never stoop to the level of a rat. You will be no contest for King Rat--he will have you for lunch!

Where to begin?

Learn from successful CEOs. They learn the most by walking around the office or the shop floor, stopping in, and chatting with individuals at lower levels in the organization. They are experts at reading upside down or looking over your shoulder. They observe networks of employees--who is visiting with whom, and for what reason.

You will find useful information by observing what goes on after hours, particularly during the evenings and on Saturdays. These are times that the King and the members of the Court come out of their burrows, frequently meeting in the open. Be friendly to the security guards, the cleaning people, the mailroom clerks, and the secretaries and administrative assistants. They have access to information that would never be put on paper, and, they are usually much better qualified for their jobs than are the executives for whom they work. Tap into the internal rumor mill. You will be surprised how much you can learn from well-placed sources in the company.

Regarding formal information, such as management compensation and perquisites--go to your company's filings with the Securities and Exchange Commission. However, be assured that useful information will be buried among the trivia, making separation of the wheat from the chaff nearly impossible. Never read the summaries--go to the full reports. Pay particular attention to exhibits, attachments, footnotes and key sentences buried in long lists of dull, apparently meaningless information. It is usually a buried, oblique reference that is the most important statement in the report. The best way to identify changes is to compare the current filing with the previous, same filing. For example, read the current Form 10-Q (Quarterly Report) side by side with the previous Form 10-Q prepared three months earlier. This will allow you to detect changes in the current submission, so you can begin questioning the meaning of that change in the disclosure. Remember, the goal of the King Rat's legal and PR team is to prevent all but those most curious and vigilant from finding relevant facts.

Information in company press releases, Internet message boards and blogs, and stock analyst reports are useless, because these are either controlled or tainted by members of the Court. In company press releases you must read between the lines to determine the real story versus the PR spin. This is not an easy exercise without direct knowledge of the event in the release. Members of the King's Court infiltrate Internet message boards and blogs. Negative information about management in such media will result in the general counsel of the company going after the poster. On the other hand, company insiders will post positive messages to counteract the negative. There will be more on stock analysts' reports later. Suffice it to say, that most of these reports are shallow and misleading.

CHAPTER 2
Chairman of the Board—"Fats"

Inbreeding of rats tends to eliminate undesirable characteristics, and to produce a homogeneous strain which is most desirable for experiments.

The Rat in Laboratory Investigation, 1949

The chairman of the board is the most important member of the King's Inner Court. The CEO cannot steal your cheese alone. He must have an accomplice who is equally committed to fraudulent behavior. The primary role of the chairman is to promote inbreeding when selecting the members of the board of directors. Inbreeding is vital for perpetuation of the species and homogeneity of the board.

In today's corporate world, there is much talk about the independence of directors. This plays well in the media, and is excellent propaganda for the rat infested company. In fact, today a King Rat is better off not being the chairman, because feigning board independence is much more cunning, and if another rat is in the chair they can work as a tag team to foil the exterminators.

ChairRat, the chairman of the board, is the fattest rat of the brood. He is grossly overweight from overfeeding and has grown lazy, as he has advanced in years. With caloric intake so out of proportion to burn rate, the pounds have added up--hence the name "Fats." Fats doesn't scamper; rather he waddles back and forth between the King Rat's office and his own on mahogany row. You see, Fats is not only very fat--he is also very old. He is the equivalent of 70 human-years, and he has spent his career devouring the cheese of several companies and building his resume in the way of King Rat. Fats is a retired King Rat, ready to act behind the scenes and teach the King with the wisdom of the ages.

Fats' former CEO positions provide him with the credibility to serve as the Chair. Because of the network that Fats has built up from defrauding others, he comes highly recommended by executive search firms, management consultants, investment bankers and politicos.

The key role of Fats is to make sure that he and King Rat maintain control of the board. He will nominate Friends of King (FOKers) and Friends of ChairRat (FOCers). Nominees have limited qualifications, proven lack of ethical standards, and appetites for the feeding that a board seat will provide. Since the members will form a social club, Fats and King are especially careful to screen out anyone who has not shown proper breeding.

Fats will put himself as the head of the nominating committee, and his closest FOCers will head the compensation committee, the finance committee and the audit committee. Most importantly, he and King will make sure to control the majority of votes on each of the committees. Board members who ask difficult questions, or who question the CEO's judgment, are branded as troublemakers and will be removed from these critical committees (Johnson 1990). These board members will find themselves on the strategy committee or the environmental sustainability committee--about which King and Fats could care less.

The nominating committee, responsible for selecting new board members, is the key position of power. King and Fats will select candidates with the "help" of an executive search firm. These searches, incredibly, end up with nominees that are in embedded relationships with Fats and King, and more incredibly, are heartily endorsed by the search firm as the most qualified candidates. This inbreeding results in boards with the appearance of independence, because of the "exhaustive" search. As George Orwell (1949,211) stated in his prophetic book *1984*, "A ruling group is a ruling group as long as it can nominate its successors."

The nominating committee will select individuals who will align their votes with King and Fats. They are preferably trophy members who sit on the board symbolically, and may be on several other boards. They have no time to review the board

materials, nor do they care to. All they are interested in is getting the money and recognition. Alternatively, they may be no-name board members who have a connection to someone who is in a position to feed the King or Fats. This type of board member depends on the board fees as a major income source. The no-names would never waiver in their allegiance to King or Fats, because they could not suffer the elimination of their compensation. Besides, being on boards is enjoyable because no work is expected (in fact work is highly discouraged) and at the same time the pay is remarkable.

Once the board is controlled, Fats' next most important task is to control the compensation committee. This committee will work closely with the head of the human resources department and with a prominent human resource consulting firm to lend an air of legitimacy to the process. The goal is to come up with a compensation package for the King bearing no resemblance to his horrendous performance. Indexing to other CEO compensation, and then positioning in the top quartile (to justify that the CEO is better than average) will ensure an upward spiral of all CEO salaries. Since most of the board members are CEOs of other companies, this has a complementary effect on their own compensation. For this result alone, the consulting fees will be well spent. As quid pro quo, to reward the board for doing such a great job, King will have the consulting firm recommend increased compensation for the board members. All are happy--the CEO becomes fabulously wealthy, the board fees go up, the board members who are CEOs of other companies receive spiraling compensation packages, and the HR consultant's fees are increased. Outside legal counsel, hired by the compensation committee, will make sure that disclosures of the compensation packages are as opaque as possible in filings required by the Securities and Exchange Commission.

Warren Buffett (2006,17), in his annual letter to the stockholders of Berkshire Hathaway, called this process "ratchet, ratchet and bingo." "Huge severance payments, lavish perks and outsized payments for ho-hum performance often occur because comp committees have become slaves to comparative data. The drill is simple: three or so directors – not chosen by chance – are bombarded for a few hours before a board meeting with pay statistics that perpetually ratchet upwards."

Fat Cats Turn to Low Fat

.....A study by the Boston Consulting Group of public companies recently found guilty of fraud calculates that the value of stock options granted to the CEOs of those firms in the years before the frauds became public was 800% greater than those granted to the CEOs of comparable firms not found guilty of any wrongdoing. Nothing correlated so strongly with corporate fraud as the value of stock options--not the standard of the firms' governance, nor analysts' inflated expectations about their earnings, nor ego-boosting stories about their CEOs in the press.

Economist March 5, 2005
Copyright 2005 by Economist Newspaper Group

The finance committee controls the purse strings of the company and establishes the rules for delegating authority to the CEO. The finance committee approves budgets, major contracts and project expenditures. Controlling the purse strings enables King and Fats to ensure that budgets, contracts and project expenditures will be based on who receives benefit, rather than what benefit the company receives. King and Fats are serving in fiduciary roles--as fiduciaries for themselves and for the FOKers/ FOCers.

Audit committees have worked in relative obscurity until the Enron debacle raised public awareness of their importance to sound governance. The independence of audit committees from management influence is critical for uncovering fraudulent practices. The audit committee of Fats' board is closely monitored and controlled by King and his chief financial officer. They will burden the committee and the committee will burden the company with meaningless paperwork providing the guise of internal controls.

With the work of the key committees fully controlled, next Fats and King choreograph the board meetings. Only members of the Inner Court will appear before the board to ensure that the board does not hear any independent thoughts. Board meetings will be held in locations remote from company facilities to avoidinadvertent contact between board members and company employees. The King and his Court will filter all

The Sky-High Club

It's tempting to wonder if the sheer prevalence of enormous C.E.O. compensation packages means that they have some beneficial effect. But academics have found little evidence that higher executive pay leads to better company performance, and the recent study of three thousand companies actually found that the firms whose directors were the most well connected – and which paid their C.E.O.s most lavishly – in fact underperformed the market.

New Yorker January 22, 2007
Copyright © 2007 The Condé Nast Publications Inc.

information to the board so that the storyline is secure. In this fashion, board members have no clue as to what is happening in the industry or in the company--as all information fed to them is for a single purpose--to extend the life expectancies of King and Fats.

Fats is in a grand position. He places FOCers on the board, and he compensates them well. King Rat makes sure that the friends of the FOCers (for mathematicians, the integral of FOCers) are well compensated by feeding off of the company's assets through contracts for consulting services, construction contracts and other supply contracts. But the prizes do not stop here. In *The Insiders*, Mark Stevens (1987) observed that some of the biggest inside traders are the corporate directors. This benefit is a welcome side-product of board membership--the "old boy network".

Fats is also in a secure position. He and King use your cheese to ensure that the directors' and officers' insurance is second to none, since this is the most important concern of the board. They spare no expense by using your cheese to hire outside advisors to attest to the board's decisions, especially those decisions that can't meet the laugh test. All of these due diligence studies have pre-arranged results (concurring with the board's decisions) to protect the board members from shareholder lawsuits.

In-between expensive company-paid travel to board junkets, Fats and the FOCers typically hang out in the rat holes of Aspen, Palm Beach, Nantucket and Fifth Avenue. Fats is so cunning and so well protected that he rarely will fall into a rattrap. Rather, Fats typically expires from cardiac arrest. His insatiable appetite for feeding on your cheese eventually clogs his arteries. This, coupled with the excitement of breeding innumerable clones of himself, usually causes death at the most inappropriate moment!

RAT PATROL

You will need to learn all that you can about the members of the board of directors to improve the precision of your **DRIAD** test results. The objective is to build the spider web of connections among the board members, management, and their friends and relatives. SEC Schedule 14A is the place to start. This provides the Proxy Statement Pursuant to Section 14(a) of the Securities and Exchange Act of 1934. It lists the names of the board members, their previous positions, and the boards on which they serve. With diligence and some detective work, you will be able to build the network of relationships among board members. It is particularly useful to understand the family tree of the board members, country club memberships and participation on nonprofit boards. Searches on the Internet will provide many clues to relationships. Don't underestimate the power of the rumor mill generated by outside suppliers and customers of the company for connecting the dots.

Board members are required to report conflicts of interests to the SEC under Regulation S-K (Disclosure of Relationships and Related Transactions). Read these conflicts carefully, and make judgments on your own as to the true "independence" of directors. Fats and King will use buffers to avoid having to report conflicts and raising red flags. Cousins and in-laws are useful for obscuring relationships.

Some words of caution...King and Fats will use company resources including the hire of private investigators to do background searches on opponents who may interfere with their feeding. If you are suspected of gaining too much knowledge, your company communications activity will be monitored. All emails will be read, Internet search activity reviewed, and voicemail scrutinized. King and Fats have spies throughout the organization, so you must be extremely careful in your research.

CHAPTER 3

Human Resources Officer—"Triple-R"

> *Adult rats are also amazingly tolerant of attempts by their young to steal food while the adults are eating it, and the young rats subsequently prefer food that they have taken from an adult's mouth to other foods they have eaten.*

> ***Encyclopedia of Animal Behavior*, 2004**

The human resources officer is a key advisor to King Rat, and is most important in stealing the cheese of employees and retirees. In great organizations, the key to success is the corporate culture set by the CEO and implemented by his human resource staff. In pathological organizations, King Rat and his Rodent Resources Rat (Triple-R) sow a culture of destruction.

King Rat knows that the best way to control a work force is through indiscriminant hiring and firing, and through employee compensation. Triple always reports directly to King, and meets privately with him more than any other member of the Court.

Rodent Resources Rat is one of the best jobs for those who receive pleasure by destroying the lives of others. She reduces or eliminates the healthcare benefits of employees and retirees who have sick spouses or children; she ensures that safety conditions in the workplace deteriorate due to neglect; she lays off dedicated employees who have given their hearts and souls to making the company a success; and she dumps employee pensions onto the Pension Benefit Guarantee Corporation once the company is approaching bankruptcy.

As suggested by the change in pronoun, Triple-R is frequently a female rat. However, "she" should be considered representative of both genders, just as any member of the King's Court may be female. Although King Rats and ChairRats are typically of the male variety, those demonstrating success in the King's Inner Court will lead to gender equality in the future. It is simply harder today for a female rat to burrow up and break through the trash ceiling.

Triple-R has two key responsibilities. Her first and most important task is to feed the King and his Court. Triple is responsible for working up salary and bonus plans, stock option agreements and other perks for King, Fats and the rest of the Inner Court. Her second task is to gather food for the King and his Court by taking it from the employees and the retirees. She will take the food right out of your mouth.

Triple-R is the primary contact with organizational consultants and compensation and benefits consultants. She hands over money to the consultants in exchange for their roles as sanitizing agents. They will be instructed to validate the King Rat's plans to eliminate employees (particularly the good ones), screw union workers out of their contractual rights, reduce benefits for salaried employees,

Bad Image for Polaroid

It's another disturbing snapshot of a corporate sale: the short-time chairman and the CEO of the Polaroid Corp. walk away with a combined payout of $21.3 million, while retirees with decades of service face the future without the healthcare and life insurance benefits they believed would always be there. So much for the once-proud image of the Waltham-based company.

The Polaroid case stings worse in some ways than other controversial corporate bankruptcies or scandals. First, the imaging company once enjoyed a stellar reputation in the field of employee benefits. Next, there is a sad banality to it all. Fraud or larceny at WorldCom, Enron, and Tyco could be laid to the criminal mind-set of corrupt executives, and criminal prosecutions provided some sense that justice would be served. But the Polaroid executives are on the up-and-up.

....

It has become almost routine for corporate executives to enrich themselves enormously while slashing jobs, forcing concessions from workers, or stripping benefits, and that's the shame.

....

"This case reflects the real divide that has emerged between senior-level executives and everybody else," says Anthony Buono, professor of management at Bentley College and a research fellow at the Waltham institution's Center for Business Ethics. "Executive compensation is out of line with reality." And too many companies, says Buono, feel no responsibility for earlier commitments to workers.

Boston Globe May 2, 2005
Copyright © 2005 Globe Newspaper Company

and eliminate retiree benefits regardless of past promises. Many of the details on how Triple-R operates will be left for the discussion of the Outer Court, since Triple rarely does anything without a consultant.

Triple works most closely with the company's general counsel to make sure that employees and retirees are treated as poorly as possible, without the company being sued excessively. If being sued becomes a problem, King and Triple work with the politicos to see that labor laws are changed or the regulatory environment is weakened to permit the pillaging.

All benefit reductions will be accompanied by propaganda stating that the survival of the firm is at stake because of the competitive global market place. "Change is required so that the company remains competitive," says King Rat. However, what is never brought up are the real reasons for the benefits cuts:

• Management never funded the healthcare promises at the time that the expenses were accrued. If they did fund these promises on a timely basis, the current competitive environment would be irrelevant to continued benefit payments. Companies built up billions of dollars of liabilities for your future healthcare. These are shown on the balance sheet as OPEB liabilities, which means the "other" postretirement employee benefit obligations of the company-- other than pensions. However, no cash was set aside in a separate fund to pay these benefits. Payment is dependent on the future success of the company. And if the company gets in trouble (which is inevitable), whatever assets remain are distributed first to the Federal government for tax obligations, second to the banks that loaned money to the company, and finally you get any crumbs that may remain since you are at the end of the line. In fact, investment bankers and private equity firms encourage high borrowing by the company in order to pull

Bosses' Pay: How Stock Options Became Part of the Problem
Once Seen as a Reform, They Grew Into Font of Riches And System
to be Gamed - Reload, Reprice, Backdate

Stock options were hailed two decades ago as a remedy for runaway executive pay. Academics, politicians and investors, tired of seeing CEOs pocket big money for a so-so job, pushed to have stock options become a primary method of compensating executives. Options – granting the right to buy stock tomorrow at today's price - would pay off only if the company's stock went up. To advocates they were the ideal carrot, an incentive for good work that aligned executives' interests with those of shareholders.

That happened – sometimes. But at many companies, options morphed into the biggest executive bonanza yet, pouring out cash like a stuck ATM, and sorely disappointing those who thought options would moderate executive pay.

Instead of replacing big bonuses, options became an additional form of pay slathered on top of already-generous packages. Employers doled out options in ever increasing numbers, in part because, until recently, accounting rules meant companies didn't have to treat this largess to executives as an expense. And...some used repricing, reloading and other tactics that made it even easier for executives to score huge hauls.

This year, options practices exploded in one of the biggest corporate-fraud scandals in decades. Some companies and executives stole from shareholders, by pretending that options had been issued earlier than they really were, at more favorable prices. At least 130 American corporations are under investigation for possible backdating of option grants. Some have admitted to it.

out more cash for themselves so that there is never anything left for you. Regarding your expectations for a pension, these obligations are required to have some funding according to government rules; however, the accounting is so arcane that King and Fats are allowed to severely underfund the pension obligations. The rat infested companies then lobby to keep the funding rules insufficient, because they are now too weak to survive if proper funding is implemented.

• The cash intended to pay for your benefits exited the company in the form of salary and bonuses to the King and his Court, and as special dividends to the owners. Your healthcare and pension funds actually do exist: they happen to be in the personal savings accounts and in the vacation homes of the King and his Court.

• Benefit cuts are necessary because of the inability of management to run a successful enterprise. You pay for the consequences of poor management.

The board and the Wall Street analysts will praise King and Triple for their ability to cut costs by eliminating you and/or your benefits.

Triple is always the first member of the Court to be assigned by King. Any hint of ethical behavior is cause for her release and replacement by a more suitable candidate. King may go through several Triple-R's before he finds one totally lacking ethics. Since the members of Triple's department serve as the executioners on behalf of King, they must ensure that none of the spilled blood can be traced back to the King.

Triple must come from a bad upbringing, as one has to be pretty sick to serve as the enforcer for the King. Indeed, the position of Rodent Resource Rat is an excellent testing ground for aspiring King Rats as her skin becomes so thick and her brain so numb that no remorse is felt. The warping of individual character

> More than 60 executives and directors of public companies have lost their jobs so far, 17 chief executive officers.
>
> *Wall Street Journal* December 27, 2006
> Copyright © 2006 Dow Jones & Company Inc.

is so advanced, that a successful Triple is a ticket to advancement in the rat kingdom. Especially since she has paid off so many consultants, her references for promotion are extraordinary!

In addition to the activities of Triple that we have discussed, the following are other methods that Triple has at her disposal to feed the King and his Court:

• All managers who are eligible for stock options sign non-compete agreements in exchange for stock option grants. They either sign the agreement or forego stock options. The gun is placed to their heads. After leaving the company, they are not allowed to work in the industry in which they are trained for up to two years. If King or Fats had such an agreement enforced at their prior company, they never would have been able to take the job in your company. The trick is a legal document called a "release". If they are in the Inner Court, Fats will release them from the non-compete agreement so that they continue feeding at another company, and pay back the favor. If they are not part of the King's Court, they will be held to the agreement to prevent them from stepping out of line.

• When the troublemakers are forced out of the Company, Triple will provide additional severance pay in exchange for an agreement that states that the former employee will never criticize the King or his Court for the rest of his or her life. No wonder so little criticism emerges from ex-employees!

•Publications to employees and retirees are typically created in Triple's department. Rest assured that the King's picture and words of wisdom are prominently displayed in every publication to show his true concern for the well-being of all employees and retirees.

•Management succession plans and evaluation plans are developed by Triple's department as a charade. The King has complete control over the outcomes, and qualifications and proven competence are not relevant criteria for promotion.

•Board compensation packages are developed with the help of consultants to ensure that the board is compensated in the upper quartile of all boards.

•Consultants and private security forces are hired to orchestrate the intimidation of union workers and to craft ways to break the unions.

•FOKers and FOCers are given lucrative consulting agreements to help advise on vital human resource matters.

•Government-mandated employee programs, such as Equal Employment Opportunity, are run by Triple's department to ensure that the letter rather than the spirit of the law is followed, and to provide a paper trail to justify the hiring of FOKers and FOCers.

•Triple out-sources benefits management to a call-center located in some remote location (or country for that matter). This ensures that the responders do not actually help the caller and further insulates the King from blame.

•Health and safety of the employees become seriously weakened.

A Special Report on Executive Pay

Right and left, Americans and Europeans, stockmarket investors and anti-globisation campaigners all share one belief: top managers pay themselves too much. The evidence seems to bear them out. For almost half a century the ratio of top executives' pay to median earnings was as smooth as a boardroom table. Then, starting in America in the 1980s and a few years later elsewhere, this ratio began to increase before taking off exponentially and peaking around the turn of the millennium. At that point the worker on an American shop floor was earning in a year what his boss on the top floor took home each evening.

Most people think they know what lay behind this. Greedy chief executives, abetted by weak, sycophantic boards, gorged themselves at the expense of savers – more often than not the very pension and mutual-fund investors who, as workers, had seen their salaries and benefit packages fail to grow.

To add to the grievance, many executives did not seem to deserve such rewards. Extraordinary pay for great performance if fine, it is routinely said. But many executives have been paid a fortune for presiding over mediocrity.

....

Companies everywhere urgently need to take steps to ensure that top executives' pay is seen as fair and deserved. That means opening it up to scrutiny and giving investors votes, rather than erecting barricades as if to hide some guilty secret. The standing of business itself is at stake.

Economist January 20, 2007
Copyright 2007 by Economist Newspaper Group

Although King and Triple pay lip service to safety, their actions and the safety record show otherwise. When major accidents occur, scapegoats will be readily available to deflect accountability away from King.

In a rat infested organization, people are not valued. They become disposable pieces of machinery. Reardon states in *The Secret Handshake* that the only way to survive in such an organization is to become "as obsequious to those in charge and to get someone else before he or she gets you" (2001,21). Since you are not a rat, such change in your ethology is unlikely. So your only alternative is to leave or to be forced out. With limited employment opportunities for those who built reputations quietly, loyally and with true humility within an organization, this is a Hobson's choice. Since you have not paid off others with company resources to find your next job, you suffer the economic consequences.

The Rodent Resources Rat will tell you in company propaganda that she is your advocate. Whenever there is an employee benefit reduction, she will spin the change to make you think that the change is actually for your benefit. Her only advocacy role is to feed the wealth and power of the King, or she would not be in her job. As long as she is stealing your cheese she can remain in the King's Court.

RAT PATROL

Human resources personnel within most companies are conduits for privileged information. They handle promotion, salary, stock options and other compensation for executives. Keep the communication channels open with members of the HR department.

The company's 10-K filing (Part III) and Proxy Statement, SEC Schedule 14A, are the places to find all of the compensation information for the top five most highly paid members of the Court. The Proxy Statement is, by far, the document most feared by the King. It exposes total compensation paid (at least that which is reported) and the growth of compensation over the past few years. By reading the 10-K (especially the exhibits) and the Proxy Statement you will be able to analyze the salaries, bonuses, stock options, pension benefits and other perks given by the board to top management. These filings also explain compensation to board members.

Compare your salary increase, or the average salary increase for the company underlings, versus those of the highest paid executives. See how the compensation package to board members has increased.

During the course of the year, keep track of the purchases and sales of company stock by these top-paid executives by reviewing SEC forms filed with each transaction. As well, read all Form 8-K submissions of your company. These will show useful information such as material definitive agreements--employment contracts, golden parachutes, and changes in stock option plans. With the Internet, review of the SEC filings is free and easy.

Pay especially close attention to the treatment of retirees of your company. A King Rat doesn't give a hoot about retirees. Although retirees are the individuals that built the assets that the King is now pilfering, he views former employees simply as liabilities to get rid of. Follow the track record of benefit changes as compared to what retirees thought that they were entitled to upon retirement--particularly in the area of healthcare benefits. The King Rat will ensure that his own healthcare is paid for in retirement, while he works to eliminate yours. Major increases in premiums, copays and deductibles, or elimination of retiree healthcare all together, are particularly devastating to lower-paid employees who believed that the company would stand behind its promises.

The outsourcing of the HR function is another sign of infestation. In this way the King Rat can distance himself from criticism. Call-center outsourcing where the responders have no clue of the benefits, or better yet, don't answer the phone, is a clear sign of trouble.

CHAPTER 4
Chief Financial Officer—"Sox"

They display a "stop-sniff-look-listen" investigation of the alley before they enter it. They then proceed up the alley at a cautious walk, with the body held low to the surface, and before reaching the food source they pause.... If they are given a large food pellet, they turn and gallop back to the refuge with the food before they eat it.

The Defensive Strategies of Foraging Rats
Psychological Record, **1991**

The chief financial officer is known as Sox. He is named after Sarbanes Oxley, the law created in response to corruption scandals attributed to weakness in financial controls. Sox has several responsibilities in the King's Court. These include managing earnings by manipulating reserve accounts and changing methods of accounting; income forecasting to make projections meet the needs of the King; overseeing investment bankers whenever churning is necessary; and providing personal financial and tax services to King, Fats and the board.

Sox' task has been made easier and more prescriptive under the provisions of Sarbanes Oxley. He is able to develop thick policy and procedure manuals to show to the auditors that accounting controls are in place. In fact, he has outside consultants do this for him to lend an air of credibility. With the help of other outside advisors, Sox finds loopholes, so that he can meet the letter but not the intent of the regulations.

Guiding the expectations of Wall Street is a prime responsibility of Sox. The goal is always to achieve movement in the stock price over the short term. King will let Sox know what the earnings are to be for a certain period. Since Sox is responsible for budgeting, he can make up earnings projections that suit the King. If the sales executives or operators don't meet the lofty goals, then they will be exterminated. Sox will find some way to mitigate the earnings variances through accounting manipulation.

Under Sarbanes Oxley, King Rat and Sox must sign the financial statements, leaving King dependent upon Sox to protect him. King is financially illiterate, so understanding financial statements is far beyond his capability. Beyond the earnings number, King doesn't care about financial statements anyway--the only question that King has for Sox is this: Are you sure that we will stay out of jail?

SEC disclosure documents are prepared by Sox with help from the company's general legal counsel and outside advisors. Whenever disclosures are made, they are accompanied by a "risks" section that is used by Sox to absolve management for the results of their incompetence. Any reasonable reading of this section would result in the conclusion that the company has so many risks that it could go out of business at any time. The section is meaningless, because the investor takes away nothing to differentiate one company versus another (Barrett 2005). The primary risk, missing from the disclosure, is having King at the helm.

Sox makes sure that corporate decisions are made on the basis of influencing short term earnings--regardless of the effect on cash flow or value of the firm. Destruction of value is acceptable if the decision results in the proper earnings impact. A favorite tactic is to sell assets that have a low cost basis because the assets may have been purchased long ago. When these assets are sold, the company will record income to make up for the shortfall from King's poor management. If the company is running short of

Read the Fine Print: We Dare You

The other day, having jaywalked back to work after knocking back a couple of cocktails, I was getting ready to operate some heavy machinery when I took a look at the latest 10-K of one of my favorite companies. Then I really got scared.

For it would seem that in post-Enron, Sarbanes Oxley era, equity investing is really risky business. SEC filings and prospectuses are chock-full of risk disclosures. There are market risks, interest rate risks, weather-related risks, product development risks, political risks, risks of not disclosing enough risk. Hey is this investing or skydiving?

Take a gander at this passage from a recent Disney filing: "For an enterprise as large and as complex as the Company, a wide range of factors could materially affect future developments and performance. These factors may include international, political, health concern, and military developments; that may affect travel and leisure businesses generally; changes in domestic and global economic conditions that may, among other things, affect the international performance of the Company's theatrical and home video releases, television programming, and consumer products; regulatory and other uncertainties associated with the Internet and other technological developments, and the launching or prospective development of new business initiatives." Yikes.

Stanford Business February 2005
Copyright © 2005 Stanford Graduate School of Business

earnings compared to what King promised the Wall Street analysts, you can be sure that there will be a fire sale of assets. These assets are sold to competitors at below market value to get them sold quickly, especially by the end of a weak financial quarter. The competitors will not only get a great deal, but they will come back to haunt when they employ the assets against King's company. But King could care less, as he will have moved on by then.

Sox is the link with bankers. Constant restructuring, merger and acquisition studies and financings help stir the pot and generate fees for the banks. The more fees the banks can earn from King's company, the better the analysts' ratings (not to mention the great mortgage rates that King and Sox receive on their vacation homes).

Chief financial officers are extremely well paid, not for their ability, but for the risk of being implicated for fraudulent behavior. Sox has many other tasks:

- Restating earnings due to past accounting errors.

- Manipulating liabilities to control earnings.

- Recording special charges to obfuscate income statement comparisons.

- Underfunding the pension plan to the maximum.

- Controlling the internal and external auditing process (despite the fact that they are auditing him).

- Approving for payment the invoices from FOKers and FOCers.

- Presenting the reasons for variances in financial performance to the board and to Wall Street analysts, so that any impairments are blamed on external factors and any improvements are due to King's great ability and vision.

- Handing out sporting event tickets to the accounting staff, and to family and friends, for the external auditor's private box.

Sox keeps the external auditors in line by increasing their fees (since additional payments to the audit firm for consulting services have been recently outlawed as bribery). Auditors have a way of justifying additional fees, as additional audit work is necessary in today's rigorous audit environment. Sox carefully watches that the areas of increased scrutiny are those areas that have already been sanitized.

In *The Transparent Leader*, Herb Baum (2004), the CEO of Dial, pointed out that legislation such as Sarbanes Oxley cannot build character in an organization. This can be accomplished only by a transparent leader who tells the whole truth.

Transparency means death to a rat.

RAT PATROL

To detect the presence of Sox, look for obfuscation of earnings releases. Whenever there is a poor financial quarter, Sox will come up with accounting changes, booked asset sales, out-of-period adjustments, reserve adjustments and all the other tricks at his disposal to come up with the earnings that the King Rat promised. The financial information is available on Form 10-Q on a quarterly basis and Form 10-K on an annual basis.

When you examine the financial statements look carefully at overhead, usually termed general and administrative expense. Companies headed by a King Rat will show rapid increases in administrative expense, particularly the amount spent on consultants, corporate aircraft, and compensation. Sox will try to bury as much of this expense in the cost of goods sold. In this way, the general and administrative expense will be understated.

Examine cost trends over several years, rather than the period-to-period comparisons provided. Sox always will show comparisons that put the company in the best light, but obscure the true story. Remember that King Rats take a profitable company and erode earnings over several years. Once earnings hit bottom, the past will be conveniently forgotten, and King will take credit for increases in earnings after they lift off the bottom.

Within the department of the chief financial officer is the tax department. Sox will work with legal counsel to find offshore tax shelters to avoid paying federal taxes. If a convenient tax deduction or credit is not available, Sox will work with the company's lobbyists to gain special provisions in the tax law. These provisions will be written in such a way

that   they
appear to be generally applicable,
but in reality, only one company meets all the criteria necessary to receive the benefit. This is the reason for targeted campaign contributions. This has nothing to do with tax fairness, but rather special interest favors in exchange for campaign financing.

Among the best sources of information to detect corporate malfeasance are the accounts payable clerks who handle the expense accounts of the executives, and who pay the bills to consultants and contractors. They pay the bills that come in from the FOKers and the FOCers. Especially interesting are unusual items that appear on the expense accounts. Be assured, however, that Sox is smart enough to assign accounting codes to such payments that are sufficiently obscure so that the auditors would never find them in routine audits.

The computer services department (often part of the CFO organization) is also a fount of knowledge. Eventually all expenses go into the computer system. These folks know the details of activities that cannot stand the light of day.

Keep your ears open whenever lunching with members of the internal audit staff, particularly those with knowledge of special investigations. However, any investigation that might lead to the CEO will go no further than Sox. It will be killed by him before it gets out of hand.

CHAPTER 5
General Legal Counsel—"Snake"

It is easy to train a rat to press a bar for food, but much more difficult and sometimes impossible to train it to press a bar to avoid shock.

Robert C. Bolles
Professor of Psychology
University of Washington, Seattle
1973

The general legal counsel is another key member of the King's Inner Court. His name is Snake, and his principal job is to protect the King Rat, Fats and the rest of the board members from civil and criminal prosecution. Although a rat's ability to avoid fatal traps is well known, with the prospect of feeding, they will withstand repeated shocks for their next meal. Snake's role is to ensure that the shock is not fatal.

Snake spends little time on what you would call "company" business. This is left to his underlings. His role is consigliere to King and Fats. He works as King' and Fats' personal attorney while his costs are expensed to the company. An exception to this rule is when working with Triple-R to reduce employee and retiree benefits without violating ERISA regulations. A second exception is his responsibility for drawing up contracts with the FOKers and FOCers to make sure that they pass the smell test.

Snake is recruited by King from outside the company, usually from the legal firm that has served as King's outside counsel. He was a marginal partner at the firm, and the other partners were happy to see him depart. In his new role, Snake will be a rainmaker by enlisting his former firm as outside legal counsel.

Snake serves as the secretary of the company to screen critical correspondence from employees and shareholders to board members. Snake is advertised as the ombudsman for the company. However, Snake reports any potential "trouble makers" to the King so that they may be targeted for elimination. As secretary, Snake also ensures that the minutes to the board meetings are meaningless, so that under discovery, an opponent would never be able to determine what occurred at a board meeting.

Revered as an expert in ethics, Snake prepares the corporate ethics guidelines, which are then issued under King's cover letter. Everyone knows that this is a charade, but the game is necessary for its propaganda value. The ethics code is enforced, but only for those outside of the King's Court.

Why Corporate Crooks are Tough to Nail

Big companies have lots of lawyers, and these lawyers specialize in creating exactly the type of paper trail that will exonerate top execs. Aggressive actions are routinely fortified with sanitizing formalities: file memos that justify iffy decisions, board approvals, and blessings from outside lawyers and accountants. Even if they helped nurture a corrupt corporate culture, CEOs and CFOs can often plausibly claim that they knew nothing about wrongdoing three or four levels down the hierarchy. All of these factors help to create the type of reasonable doubt that kills criminal prosecutions. In the Enron case, Lay, Skilling, and Fastow are all likely to argue that the company's disclosures were approved by Andersen. "They're going to say, `Look, I'm not an accountant. I told them what I wanted to do, and they said it was O.K.,'" says Houston criminal and civil defense attorney David Berg.

Business Week July 1, 2002
© *2002* by The McGraw-Hill Companies, Inc.

[Author's Note: Lay, Skilling and Fastow **were** nailed! Ken Lay was convicted in 2006, but his conviction was vacated when he died later that year; Jeff Skilling, serving a 24-year prison sentence, learned in January 2009 that a federal appeals court upheld his conviction but ordered resentencing that will likely cut several years off his time in the slammer; and Andy Fastow is serving a six-year prison sentence and is scheduled for release in 2011.]

Ethics guidelines will not succeed if those involved do not have basic moral inclinations (Aguilar 1994). "When we leave honesty out of ethics we get hypocrisy. That's why so many so-called codes of ethics are ineffective," said Ivan Hill in his essay "The Meaning of Ethics and Freedom" (1976,7). "If the codes are not internalized and manifested in individual behavior, the codes will have little impact on the acculturation of individuals in the industry... A code of 'ethics' may be no more than a legalistic gloss over the real ethos that pervades the organization", said Professor Dobson (2003,29) in "Why Ethics Codes Don't Work."

As you can see, Snake's true function can be compared to products that turn water blue in your toilet, such as Tidy Bowl. His job is to sanitize the actions of the King and his Court so that they can withstand challenge. He makes sure that the formalities are followed to obey the letter of the law, while crushing the spirit. He uses law firms in the King's Outer Court to legitimatize the process and lend credence to the results. Snake becomes so tainted in the process, that he can never turn on King, ever, or he would be disbarred and jailed. Hence, Snake's loyalty to King is secured forever.

RAT PATROL

To detect Snake's presence, examine the disclosures made by the company in the SEC filings. If you find these disclosures to be so obtuse as to be meaningless, then Snake is lurking in the tall grass. You must be able to read between the lines in any public document. The words will be chosen to sanitize the document, and to mislead the reader from knowing the truth, without telling an outright lie.

Legal counsel also will recommend organizational structures to create off-balance sheet financing (à la Enron) to understate the borrowings of the firm. Snake will develop complicated organizational structures to create tax havens, hide liabilities, and shield assets from creditors. Snake is particularly adept at labor law, to ensure that the workforce is controlled and monitored. As well, assets will be split off from any corporation that may have large liabilities to union workers. Snake's techniques would not be possible without the help of favorable legislation passed by the politicos.

CHAPTER 6
Public and Investor Relations Officer—"Spin"

We can neither assert nor deny discontinuity between human and subhuman fields so long as we know so little about either. If, nevertheless, the author of a book of this sort is expected to hazard a guess publicly, I may say that the only differences I expect to see revealed between the behavior of rat and man (aside from enormous differences in complexity) lie in the field of verbal behavior.

B.F. Skinner
The Behavior of Organisms
1938

The public and investor relations officer is the outside world's window into the company. The King only allows this one window to be open, as the picture viewed through this window is quite different from the general state of the company. Spin's role is self-descriptive, he is to spin all news coming out of the company to achieve two objectives: to keep the stock price as high as possible until King and Fats can cash out their options; and, to make King appear to be the best chief executive officer in all the world. Spin has the most difficult job among the members of the Court. His creativity must be second to none--his sophistry impeccable. He is the mouthpiece for the company, providing the verbal behavior that B.F. Skinner claimed to be the only true difference between humans and rats.

Under his public relations role, Spin produces the company

newspaper, publicity brochures and the annual report. With regal splendor, the greatness of the King and his Court is woven throughout the publications. Spin fabricates all of the King's direct quotes and prominently displays the King's name and picture for any contributions, civic activities or events sponsored with company funds. Whenever company publications change from black and white to color, and the King's pictures increase in size and frequency, these are warning signs of infestation.

Spin is responsible for the ubiquitous press releases. If the press release is presenting favorable news (which is rare), King is quoted. If the news is negative, Spin works with Snake to make sure that the press release meets SEC disclosure guidelines, but obfuscates the true problems. Nowhere will King be in the picture.

If the King is not quoted in a favorable press release, he is setting up someone to fail. For example, when King wants a temporary spike in the stock price, he may announce a project that he knows will not go forward. In this case, the quote will be ascribed to someone outside the Inner Court. Thus, when the project does not materialize, he will have someone to blame for the failure.

Whenever the press wants a quote from the company, it is invariably from Spin. The King would never want anyone else in the spotlight, because Spin is the only one who knows the story line. If you are not telling the truth, sticking to the same story becomes quite difficult unless the outlet is limited to a single storyteller. The others might slip and tell the truth. Spin has the experience to walk the tightrope. The words that he writes and the quotes that he makes literally have a shade of truth that would be defendable in court. However, any reasonable person would be misled by the words--after all, that is the goal of King and Spin. Few in the public realm have ever seen a King Rat in person, because he operates in darkness. Spin is all that is needed to create the illusion that King is indispensable.

In some companies, Spin wears a second hat--as the Investor Relations Rat. He works with Wall Street analysts and institutional buyers of the stock to make sure that they bite on the company story line. To do this, Spin usually makes up a strategy for the company and presents this strategy on PowerPoint slides. Little do they know, but there is nothing behind the slides except for Spin's creativity. Long-term strategy is irrelevant to King, except to convey to the analysts and the investment community that he is operating with a plan that is favorable to the Street.

It works like this. Spin finds out what Wall Street analysts and institutional investors want to hear about the future, and then he formulates the story. This becomes the adopted strategy, until the fickle Street reverses its views. Then the plan is changed (frequently 180 degrees) to accommodate the latest views from the outsiders. All decision-making in the company is based on the following question: What will Wall Street think, and how will it move the stock in the short term?

Since Spin has no idea of future financial performance, he

gets this information from Sox. Sox will feed him only what King wants to tell in order to drive the stock in one direction or another. You see, King is telling his friends when to buy and sell.

Spin meets regularly with the Wall Street analysts. He feeds them assumptions for their financial models that result in the story that King wants to tell. The analysts are typically young and inexperienced, so they accept Spin's assumptions and amazingly come up with the same conclusions in their reports. In exchange, the analysts' brokerage houses will continue to receive investment banking business from King and Sox.

Spin and the other members of the King's Court are known as Potemkin authorities--defined as those who faithfully spout the opinions of their benefactors while making it appear that their views are independent (Rampton and Stauber 2001).

During the reign of Catherine the Great in Russia, one of her closest advisors was Field Marshal Grigori Potemkin. When Catherine toured the countryside with foreign dignitaries, Potemkin arranged to have fake villages built in advance of her visit. These villages created the illusion of prosperity in the kingdom. A Potemkin village has become a metaphor for things that look elaborate and impressive, but in reality, lack substance.

Spin's job simply stated is to create a Potemkin village for the investment community's view of the company. Spinning is the art of appearance over substance. The practitioners of public relations in rat infested companies do not falsify the truth, because they do not believe that truth exists.

George Orwell provided remarkable training for Spin. The parallel between George Orwell's "Newspeak" and the behavior of the modern Investor and Public Relations Rat is too close for coincidence. It is amazing to watch a talented Spin eliminate all real knowledge of a company by working with King to wipe

Make Room on the PR-Plate to Enhance Business Ethics

"Ethics is the foundation for a successful economy. It isn't optional," says Linnea McCord, an associate professor of business law at the Graziado School of Business and Management, Pepperdine University.... Pr execs have to "help the CEO understand the essential importance of ethics and how ethical conduct impacts the bottom line, which can quickly go from black to red," McCord adds.

PR News February 9, 2004
Copyright © 2004 Access Intelligence, LLC.

[Author's Note: In a company led by a King Rat, if a PR exec tried to "help him understand the importance of ethics", I suspect that the result would not be pretty. The King Rat's message in reply would be, "leave your keys on your desk, and don't let the door hit you on the way out."]

out institutional memory. The true purpose of Newspeak is to narrow the range of thought so that there is no need to think independently. This is called the "mutability of the past"--the denial of objective reality (Orwell 1949,214). Analysts, investors and employees eventually tolerate the present conditions because all standards of comparison are eliminated. After a few years, all knowledge of the past is wiped out, and the King is free to set his own standards.

King Rat is presented by Spin to be omnipotent and infallible. Since this is balderdash, Spin must introduce what Orwell called "blackwhite". In Orwellian Newspeak, the loyal are willing to say that black is white when the King decrees that this is so. "It means also the ability to believe that black is white, and to know that black is white, and to forget that anyone has ever believed the contrary" (ibid.,213).

Orwell also introduced Spin to "doublethink"--the power of holding two contradictory beliefs in one's mind simultaneously and believing in both of them. Spin will "be conscious of complete truthfulness while telling carefully constructed lies" (ibid.,36). On occasion, a successful Spin has been known to advance to the position of King, as doublethink is a necessary skill of a King Rat.

As Harrington (1959) stated in *Life in the Crystal Palace*, the process of doublethink must be conscious or it could not be carried out with precision, but it also must be unconscious or it would bring on a sense of guilt. You may ask the question, "How can the King and his Court carry on with the guilt that they must bear?" The answer is--there is no guilt in the mind of a rat.

The art of spinning has become known as the intentional manipulation of the truth. Spinning is not the truth and it is not an outright lie. However, when spinning is used to deceive, cover-up and to distort the facts, it becomes lying (Press 2001). Spin, in the practice of spinning, must be careful to ensure that he does not tell a lie that can be proven.

Orwellian Newspeak, especially blackwhite and doublethink, is a required second language for anyone training to become the Investor and Public Relations Rat in the King's Court. B.F. Skinner said that verbal behavior is the only difference between rat and man--and Spin provides that verbal behavior for the King and his Court.

Where Were the PR Wizards?

Nowhere, in the torrents of media reporting and analyses of the Enron era shenanigans, have the PR chiefs been mentioned—not as co-conspirators, not even as dupes—and they were the principal conduit to the public of the misleading information.

One wonders what the resplendent titles mean: Tyco vice president of corporate communications; Enron vice president of public relations plus four vice presidents of communications and five directors of public relations reporting to him. Other companies tainted by scandal—Global Crossing, Dynergy, WorldCom, Qwest—also had managers with lofty titles, from executive vice president to senior VP to plain-vanilla vice presidents. None were mentioned in the dispatches from the front. (Arthur Andersen put public relations under a vice president of finance. Figures.)

Two exceptions related to the broiling scandals: The PR chief to SEC chairman Harvey Pitt made the news as the counselor who prodded Pitt to seek a raise and cabinet status at the height of his beleaguered tenure. (He has since resigned.) And Tyco shunted its communications VP aside and hired an image-polisher whose game plan was to transform CEO Dennis Kozlowski into a Jack Welch look-alike.

Across the Board May 1, 2003
Copyright 2003 by Conference Board Inc.

RAT PATROL

If Spin is truly effective, you will be unable to detect his presence. You will need to be knowledgeable of the rules of propaganda whenever reading a publication generated by Spin or listening to his prepared speeches.

Signs of trouble: Large pictures of the King Rat in annual reports and company publications; glorification of the King Rat for company successes; no sign of the King Rat during times of trouble (he is unavailable for comment); and creation of Potemkin villages, when you know better.

CHAPTER 7
Corporate Development Officer—"Squealer"

A rat attempting to steal food nearly always approaches a feeding rat from the rear.

The Defensive Strategies of Foraging Rats
Psychological Record, 1991

The corporate development officer may be called by a variety of titles depending on the company. He may be the head of administration, the head of planning, the head of business development, or the head of strategy. He is the utility infielder for the King--playing any position that the King needs to carry out his feeding. Any job that doesn't neatly fit within the realm of Triple-R, Sox, Snake or Spin is a job for Squealer.

Squealer is a particularly vicious rat, as he is hand-picked by King to be his understudy. He must have the characteristics that will enable him to become a future King, and he is put to the test at a young age to evaluate his fitness. His primary role is to help the King cleanse the company of anyone who might stand in the way of the King's feeding. He carries out the dirty work for the King, so that the King's hands remain unbloodied. He rarely confronts fellow employees from the front, but prefers to stab them in the back under the instruction and the watchful eye of the King.

Squealer is named after the pig in George Orwell's (1954)

Animal Farm. Since the King is rarely seen in the flesh, Squealer is the proxy for King in conducting company business. He speaks for the King within the company, and is present to carry out the King's wishes. In many ways he serves in the position of master of ceremonies. He throws softballs to the King, intercepts the hardballs, runs interference, finds out who speaks poorly of the King, and justifies the King's actions.

In *Power Shift*, Alvin Toffler (1990,199) best described the relationship between Squealer and King: "The vassal is dependent on the lord who is higher up. Yet the top dog can be totally dependent on the underling, whose chief unofficial function is to conceal from others the weakness of the boss."

The following are the primary activities of Squealer:

- Negotiates agreements with the FOKers and FOCers who are given lucrative vendor contracts with the company. In order to give the illusion of no conflict of interest, the King never signs his name to such a contract.

- Prepares budgets and financial projections that bear no resemblance to the input from operations and sales. These budgets and plans are established to hit the numbers set out by the King for wooing Wall Street. If the line managers don't meet the targets, the King fires them for not meeting the objectives.

- Prepares management reviews and post-audits of past decisions. He rewrites history to place any blame on the King's predecessors or any current opponents of the King. All blame is directed away from the King. He controls the records department so that lies become truths.

- Controls the purchasing department of the company, so that the FOKers and FOCers know what to bid to get the business.

- Coordinates the activities of management consultants to ensure

The Making of the Neo-KGB State
The Inner Circle

As the new president [Vladimir Putin] saw things [in 1999], his first task was to restore the management of the country, consolidate political power and neutralize alternative sources of influence: oligarchs, regional governors, the media, parliament, opposition parties and nongovernmental organizations. His KGB buddies helped him with the task.

The most politically active oligarchs...were pushed out of the country, and their television channels were taken back into state hands.

To deal with unruly regional governors, Mr. Putin appointed special envoys with powers of supervision and control. Most of them were KGB veterans. The governors lost their budgets and their seats in the upper house of the Russian parliament. Later the voters lost their right to elect them.

All strategic decisions...were and still are made by the small group of people who have formed Mr. Putin's informal politburo.

Economist August 25, 2007
Copyright 2007 by Economist Newspaper Group

that their conclusions fit the predetermined outcomes desired by the King.

• Prepares glossy PowerPoint presentations to the board of

directors to channel the board discussion, to establish blame for poor performance and to provide cover for the King.

With such far-reaching responsibilities, Squealer is different from Sox, Triple, Snake and Spin because he has access to each of their individual functions...and he is the King's internal spy. If any members of the Court become too independent, Squealer will make sure that the King is informed so that corrective action is taken.

Jeremy Bentham's design of the Panopticon is the best model for Squealer's organizational oversight. Bentham's Panopticon was a 19th century prison designed to control the inmates. Its configuration was a circular building with a central observation tower from which the inmates could be observed without being able to observe the observers (Moore 2000). The philosopher Foucault discussed Panopticism in understanding modern organizations--where humans are normalized (Burrell 1988). King with Squealer's aid establishes discipline in the organization in a Panopticonian manner. The geometry of control in the organization is vital for maintaining discipline and exposing potential troublemakers.

The recent advancements in communications and computer technology enable surveillance of employees in an unprecedented manner. The Fourth Amendment to the Constitution provides no protection to the employee of a corporation. Employers can, and do, monitor phone calls as long as they are in the ordinary course of business. They review phone logs, voice mails, emails, and Internet usage and use surveillance cameras. In *The Naked Employee*, Lane (2003) stated that 12% of US corporations periodically record and review telephone calls and 8% store and review voice messages. Forty-three percent monitor the amount of time that employees spend on the phone and check the phone numbers that are called.

Forty percent periodically search computer files.

There are no reliable statistics on employer wiretapping of employees or the planting of secret bugs in their offices. Although illegal, such methods are in the toolkit of the King Rat.

Email has no privacy whatsoever, as all emails are stored. New programs are being used to screen all emails for key words, such as King Rat, Fats, stealing, lying, and cheating. This email scanning software can be customized for each company, so the King Rat is able to call up all emails that have potential to inflict harm on him. If you are considered a threat to the King, no doubt all of your emails are being reviewed.

In a survey by the American Management Association, 60% of employers said that they monitor employees' email (Tam et al 2005). This new software can track every single keystroke. Companies are reporting that they have increased staffing to read employee email. About the only place you are safe is in the rest room (and indeed the bathroom stalls may be monitored in the rat infested company). To maintain power the King will eliminate or severely restrict privacy rights of employees. Employees have limited protection from the King Rat who may not like what was said online.

As Squealer is being groomed, King and Fats ensure that Squealer is given high visibility with the board and with Wall Street. The evidence from psychology, anthropology, sociology and ethology strongly favors Squealer to become a CEO. In the natural selection process, those who follow the most successful models to imitate are the most favored to survive and prosper (Gil-White 2000).

Squealer needs significantly more training before he is ready to assume the role of King Rat. As with all members of the Inner Court, none are capable of taking the King's position while he is still feeding. This would be too dangerous for the King. In fact, Squealer will not be ready until the King Rat hits 65 years of age in human-years.

RAT PATROL

Detection of Squealer is easy. Everyone in the company knows the identity of Squealer. Whenever Squealer speaks, he is doing so on behalf of the King.

Squealer quickly builds a reputation as a back-stabber. He is feared by honest employees, and he is worshiped by aspiring rats. Squealer is in every meeting of importance, as he is the spy for the King Rat. If he is not invited, he invites himself. Squealer becomes paranoid if he believes that he is out of the information loop.

A log of his telephone calls (not easy to obtain) would show that he is in constant communication with those who can provide benefit to the King and Fats. King tells him who should be given contracts with the company. Squealer signs these contracts to avoid appearances of conflict of interest.

Although everyone knows Squealer, his modis operandi remains secret. His door will never be open to prevent others from seeing with whom he is meeting and to avoid eavesdropping by others. His itinerary is a secret, and he travels extensively. He sets up meetings with FOKers and FOCers in discrete locations to avoid sightings by company insiders. He spends much of his time in the presence of the King Rat, especially in corporate aircraft, limousines, and lodging whenever King is on the move.

Section II

The Outer Court

*The rat, of course, I rate first [in intelligence among animals].
He lives in your house without helping you buy it or build it or
repair it or keep the taxes paid; he eats what you eat without
helping you raise it or buy it or even haul it into the house; you
cannot get rid of him; were he not a cannibal, he would long
since have inherited the earth.*

The Reivers: A Reminiscence
William Faulkner
1897-1962

The King Rat is supported by ten categories of outside organizations and individuals. In many instances there may be several companies or individuals in a category. However, the commonality of these organizations is their inhabitation by Friends of King and Friends of ChairRat (the FOKers and FOCers).

When outside entities are introduced to the CEO of a potential client company, they quickly identify whether they are dealing with a King Rat. Companies led by a King are the most lucrative clients, because fees do not matter. In fact, the higher the fees the better, since the King uses the Outer Court to spread your cheese to third parties, and the more cheese he spreads around, the more popular he becomes as a CEO.

The members of the Outer Court jockey for position by being client-centric--this means serving the King rather than the best interests of the company. Any outsider who does not get the message, or is too honest to accept this role, will be excluded from the feast. The ten most influential members of the Outer Court provide the means for the King to maintain power, while at the same time enriching themselves at your expense.

CHAPTER 8

Management Consultant—
"Ratti and Company"

> *Strongyloides ratti, a nematode that, as the name suggests, lives inside of rats. The females living in the guts of rats lay eggs without any help from males. Once these eggs leave the rat's body they hatch and their larvae emerge as one of two different forms. One form is all female, and it spends its time looking for a rat to penetrate. It gets into the skin of the rat and then glides through it until it reaches the rat's nose. There it finds the nerve endings that the rat uses to smell, and follows them into the brain. From there the parasite takes a route – no one knows the details – all the way to the rat's intestines, and starts making female clones again.*
>
> **Parasite Rex: Inside the Bizarre World of**
> **Nature's Most Dangerous Creatures, 2000**

Ratti and Company is representative of prominent management consulting firms. Its partners live in the gut of a King Rat and quickly make their way to his brain (if it can be found). In time, Ratti becomes the brains of the company, as no major strategic decision is made without its advice. Once inside the company, the parasitic cycle is underway. Over $20 billion per year is spent on management consulting (Kihn 2005). This is amazing--when you consider the compensation of King Rats, who are presumably hired for their strategic abilities. Why do they need over $20 billion every year for handholding?

That, however, is a naïve question. The reason why management consulting is so lucrative is not because King and Fats want to improve the company for the shareholders--rather they want protection. King and Fats hire Ratti to protect themselves and the board of directors from criticism and lawsuits.

The game is played like this. Typically your company stock is reeling due to poor management decisions (or the lack of management decisions). King Rat needs to make a showing to Wall Street that he is in control of costs. However, King has no clue how the company runs, or, who the people are within the company that drive the results. He does not stoop to this level of detail since he would become too confused and he would not be able to solve the problems anyway.

Thus, he invites in several management consulting firms for interviews. They all show him how they can cut overhead by 30 percent and drive profits by their trademark methods. These presentations, just like Squealer's, are always on PowerPoint slides. These slides are fungible, and may be used for any client. If the management consultant does not present what the CEO wants (which is unlikely because Squealer instructed its partner-in-charge in advance), then they revise their presentation to satisfy the King's wishes.

The King then hires one of the management consultants with a high profile name and a fee structure that is even higher. Since the consultant's fees will run in the millions, King knows that this will impress the board and the investment community.

Hiring Ratti is what consultants call a win-win. Ratti wins by securing a lucrative contract. King wins by putting on a show for the board and Wall Street, keeping any critics at bay so that he can buy more time as CEO. His only interest is to survive until the next quarter. King stays alive on a quarter-by-quarter basis. When the King's time is finally up in the company, the management consultant is sure to provide a superb reference for the King. The only loser in this game is you--the employee, the retiree, and the shareholder.

At the beginning of an engagement, King will send out an announcement about how the consultant is being brought in to analyze the strengths and weaknesses of the company and to provide "best practices." However, the truth is that King brought them in because they are smart enough to know the answers that King wants, and they deliver those answers for a price. Ratti's partners know who approves their invoices--and it's not you. This is the last time the employees will hear from the King or see Ratti's partner-in-charge of the engagement. From now on Squealer will run the show with Ratti's associates who are brought in from around the globe.

Ratti knows little about the business of your company. No problem. Ratti hires freshly minted MBAs from high-profile business schools who have been trained to learn any business in a week. These associates become nematodes in the organization. They fly in from their distant homes, arrive on a Monday   afternoon, work well into the   night   in   a   secluded conference   room inputting   data into

proprietary computer programs, and leave on Thursday evening to return to places such as New York, Chicago or Dallas.

The behavior of the consultant is closely tied to the ethology of the King. In a rat infested company, the management consultant acts as a political agent for the King (Van Es 2002). As political agent, Ratti aids and abets King's intentional and repeated inflictions of physical and psychological harm on the employees of the company (Vandekerckhove 2003). A study in the *Journal of Business Ethics* tested the effects of individual values and professional ethics of the consultant on his or her consulting behavior. The study determined that there is no relationship (Allen and Davis 1993).

Having observed management consultants for over three decades, what became apparent to me was the similarity of their playbooks. Indeed, I observed that their methods were borrowed from those used by corrupt regimes on prisoners, and even on their own people.

These tactics are the same used by the North Korean Army on American prisoners in the early 1950's and by Mao Ze Dong on the Chinese people during the Cultural Revolution in the 1970's. Their methods are cunning, cruel and effective. They are based on empowering employees within the organization to become prison guards. Employees are forced to recommend the elimination of their colleagues--so that the blood is not on the hands of King or Ratti.

It works like this. As the appointed controlling authority, Ratti establishes the context for the exercise, and unless one can break through that context, the end result is inevitable. For example, the consultant may say that overhead must be reduced by 30 percent. Then, department heads must come up with ways to achieve this goal for their departments. The context is not to be challenged. The consultants will target FTE's (full time equivalent positions), never human beings. Similar to high level bombing--their objective is to kill in a sanitary way.

Stanley Milgram (1974) showed how easy it is to manipulate the thinking and behavior of others by using false experts. In his 1974 study, *Obedience to Authority*, Milgram reported on experiments that he conducted in the early 1960's in the Psychology Department of Yale University. An experimenter ordered participants in the study to deliver what they thought to be increasingly stronger electric shocks to a person strapped into an electric chair in an adjoining room. Those administering the shocks could hear the crying and moaning of those they thought were being shocked. About two-thirds of the participants delivered what they must have thought were highly painful and even deadly shocks.

Obedience to Authority is the gospel of the management consultant crowd. Milgram's fundamental lesson was that "ordinary people, simply doing their jobs, and without any particular hostility on their part, can become agents of a terrible destructive process" (ibid.,6). He emphasized that in large institutional structures, such as governments and major companies, it is inevitable that man abandons his humanity as he merges his personality into that of the institution.

Milgram argued that subjects find it difficult to act out of context, and that the power of context to shape human behavior is overlooked consistently (Bella, King and Kailin 2003). This profound statement is what allows King Rats to set the context and maintain their positions of power.

The Stanford Prison Experiment by Professor Phillip Zimbardo in 1971 showed the potential for abusing underlings by those given positions of power. Zimbardo halted his experiment prematurely due to escalating guard brutality after six days rather than the planned two weeks (Zimbardo 2006). The management consultant, fronting for the King, establishes the context and carries out the abuses that result in the outcome desired by the King.

Huxley (1958) in *Brave New World Revisited* described the methods used by the Chinese Communists on military prisoners. The prisoners were required to write about their sins and those of their companions in order to intensify their guilt. They were subjected to systematic stress. The goal was to create a climate where everyone was spying on each other. Similar techniques were used to enforce Communism in China. Members of the Party were sent to a special camp, always in groups, and were encouraged to spy on one another, and to write about their personal weaknesses.

You are not to think for yourself. You must follow the philosophy of the King and his consultant. Those who question the authority are branded as troublemakers, not team players, and are rapidly excluded from the process (Rasiel 1999). These are the individuals who are labeled as being inflexible, unwilling to change, and stuck in doing things the old way. In my experience, these are typically the most skilled and talented individuals, and they are the troublemakers. They know far more than the consultants, become obstacles to the consultants, and are capable of embarrassing the consultants. They are unwilling to accept the context established by the consultants.

Ratti and fellow management consultants are context creators and break down the resistance of normal, well-adjusted employees. They believe in *The Big Lie* (Rampton and Stauber 2001)--the bigger the lie, the more people will believe it. They dazzle with information and statistics--most of which is meaningless at best, or misleading at worst. Management consultants are hired to

Survey: Why Honesty is the Best Policy
Corporate Deceit is a Slippery Slope

For every corporate crook there are at least ten corporate deceivers: people who fool themselves that things are other than what they appear to be. At first they do not break the law, but eventually they find that corporate deceit is difficult to sustain. "Oh what a tangled web we weave when first practise to deceive." wrote Sir Walter Scott in 1808.

....

Above all, though, consultants loved [Enron]. In "The War for Talent" (Harvard Business School Press, 2001), Ed Michaels, Helen Handfield-Jones and Beth Axelrod wrote that: "Few companies will be able to achieve the excitement extravaganza that Enron has in its remarkable business transformation, but many could apply some of the principles."

Economist March 9, 2002
Copyright 2002 by Economist Newspaper Group

systematically distort information to achieve the desired result of the King. Distortions that benefit the King and his Court involve tremendous transfers of wealth.

Ratti's conclusions, just like their proposals, are given in PowerPoint presentations, with minimal words, but lots of diagrams and pictures (Rasiel 1999). Analysis is not provided to prevent others from seeing through the weakness of the consultant's conclusions. The consultant will claim that his analysis is proprietary. In fact, it is fiction. If anyone dares to ask a consultant a tough question, he turns it around and asks the client's opinion or attempts to flatter the client (Kihn 2005). They are always working within their model, which gives their analysis an aura of legitimacy.

In the end, the consultant comes up with the body count and the recommended organizational structure. Then they turn the process over to Triple-R to take care of those

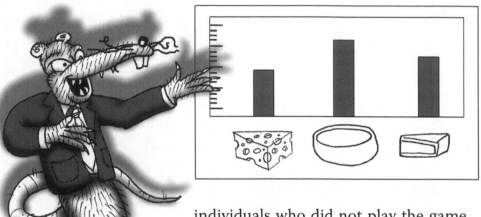

individuals who did not play the game. The brightest and the best are banished, as these are the individuals who saw through the charade and were unwilling to compromise their ethical standards. For this they are shot. They will be offered assignments in far-off places, shunted to the side, or simply eliminated by the "reduction in force."

During the Great Proletarian Cultural Revolution from 1966 to 1976, Mao and his wife Jiang Qing, destroyed the bureaucracy, paralyzed education and research, and left the economy of China in shambles. Mao encouraged students to join the Red Guard, which persecuted teachers and intellectuals (Hoffmann 1971). The Cultural Revolution was Mao's self-defense in protecting Communism. Professors from the universities were sent to the farms to do physical labor and for "reeducation."

At the enterprise level, efforts were made to prevent personal power from becoming too strong (Laaksonen 1984). Similarly, Ratti's consulting engagement is King's self-defense in protecting himself, particularly against those who may challenge him. Ratti's recommendations for reorganization will target for elimination those with independent thoughts.

In *Power Shift*, Toffler (1990) spoke of the three sources of power as being violence, wealth and knowledge. Although the consultant's overt mission is to increase the efficiency of the company, the true mission is for management to gain control through the consultant. Toffler's rationale for why violence is so rare in business today is because it is contracted out to the consultants and the lawyers.

The assignment of Ratti to improve the efficiency of the company is now concluded. King has no blood on his hands, nor does Ratti. The consultants take a well-deserved cruise in the Mediterranean before taking on the next bloodletting. The King has eliminated his foes, and basks in the glory of Wall Street.

But after a few weeks of rest and relaxation, Ratti's partner-in-charge once again appears in the corner office to meet with King. In this meeting, the follow-up phases of the consultant's work program are presented. Additional assignments are necessary to ensure that Ratti's income projections from the first phase of the engagement are achieved:

- If the income goes down after the consulting assignment, it shows that Ratti was not given sufficient follow-up contracts to monitor progress. Invariably, Ratti comes up with recommendations for information technology systems (very expensive), changing methods of materials management (a fancy name for purchasing), operational changes and strategic planning systems. Hence, the first study blossoms into several more. The increase in consulting fees paid by the company is justified since 30% of the overhead has been cut. Since the internal capability has been depleted, the consultants are now actually needed! The performance suffers, but that only means opportunity for King and Ratti. A new consulting engagement will recommend adding back the positions that were cut; however, now King can fill the jobs with FOKers and FOCers.

- If the income goes up after the assignment, the reasons usually can be attributed to market factors outside of the company's control. However, King will take full credit for the gain, and put Ratti on permanent retainer. King can "lunch" on a monthly basis with Ratti's partners to gain their wisdom.

King Rat never has the ability to manage the company without the help of consultants. In fact, he couldn't manage a two-chair barbershop with the other barber on vacation. Why does the board pay him millions of dollars if he doesn't know how to manage a company? The answer is simple--the objective is not to better manage the company, it is all about feeding the board rats.

RAT PATROL

The way that management uses outside consultants, particularly general management consultants, will tip off the presence of Ratti. Be particularly aware of consultants who provide services that should be within the core capabilities of the company--such as strategy, planning, purchasing, and operations. If you are within a firm infiltrated by management consultants, be cognizant of prisoner of war tactics. Remember, when engaged by a King Rat, the consultant is a political agent. Understanding the consultant's true role will make sense of the tactics that you observe during their assignment. Always see through the context that they are attempting to set. But don't be brash or you will be labeled a troublemaker and exiled to do hard labor in the countryside.

CHAPTER 9

Outside Legal Counsel—"Serpente, Timador, Incallidus, Nulo, Klepto and Yashtsherke LLP"

Rat snakes alter their action patterns depending on the prey. Rat snakes do not constrict small prey if they can be easily swallowed. Whereas large prey would be automatically constricted. The ability to change prey handling techniques to match the difficulty of the prey is advantageous because constriction appears energy intensive.

Rat Snake—*Elaphe obsoleta*
***Encyclopedia of Animal Behavior*, 2004**

Outside legal counsel serves as an extension of Snake, the company's General Legal Counsel. Attorneys Serpente, Timador, Incallidus, Nulo, Klepto and Yashtsherke formed this limited liability partnership. The law firm is commonly referred to simply as Serpente or by the acronym Stinky LLP. Serpente has an outward appearance of sanctimony; however, it will crush its prey (expending as little energy as possible) at the beckoning of the King. The firm is mercenary, attacking the enemies of the King in exchange for greenbacks.

Serpente works in three principal areas. The first is to provide expert counsel on compensation agreements for the King and his Court. Second, it ensures that the company meets the letter of the law, and SEC and stock exchange regulations. Third, it defends the officers and directors from lawsuits, and intimidates the opponents of King and Fats.

Serpente's attorneys work with Triple-R, Snake and the board's compensation committee to provide employment contracts, equity incentive plans, and golden handshake and golden parachute agreements. Presumably they are working on behalf of the board when developing such plans; however, King drives the process.

Legitimatizing the actions of management and the board as they are stealing your cheese is an important role. King never wants to be told that he cannot do what he wants to do. Serpente's role is to tell him how to do it (Atkinson 2004). The firm has particular expertise on how management can receive perks while avoiding disclosure in SEC documents, or by obfuscating disclosure. No expense is spared for

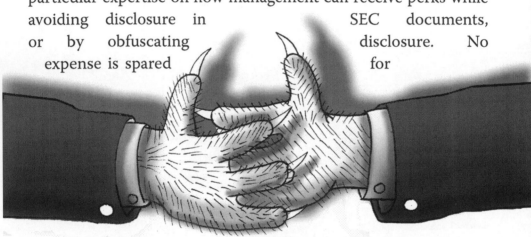

an opinion that the actions of management and the board are considered legal. Serpente validates financial maneuvers that have no legitimate business purpose, exploits loopholes in the tax law and financial disclosure regulations, and when the law is unfavorable, prepares language to change the law to advantage its client. Within this latter category is the role played by Serpente to weaken labor relations law. The law firm will help its clients bust unions, diminish employee benefits and weaken worker protection.

Interested Parties: In Internal Probes of Stock Options Conflicts Abound

...The donations were just one instance of overlapping relationships and potential conflicts of interest that exist at some companies conducting investigations of their own stock-option practices. The various relationships don't necessarily mean board members can't be fully objective. But governance experts warn that, at the least, the ties are likely to hinder public confidence in the thoroughness of the inquires.

With options under scrutiny at more than 80 companies so far, regulators and prosecutors haven't the resources to conduct full-blown forensic probes of every company. They often rely on companies' own internal inquiries to do the initial digging that helps authorities decide whom to pursue most vigorously. In addition, the companies themselves rely on these internal probes, either to show the public they've been diligent or to defend against shareholder suits.

In these probes, "if the government catches wind of issues affecting independence, they will naturally be more skeptical and less trusting of the process and the results," said W. Scott Sorrels, an Atlanta attorney who has conducted investigations for corporate boards in the past. Mr. Sorrels, not speaking of any firm, said: "We advise companies to avoid any appearance of impropriety so you don't have the situation blow up in your face six months down the road after the investigation is done."

Wall Street Journal August 11, 2006

Serpente defends the company, its officers and directors from shareholder lawsuits and from litigation stemming from the misdeeds of the company. Indeed, we have Serpentes on both sides of these cases to steal your cheese as a shareholder or as a claimant against the company. There is no shortage of Serpentes given the fabulous wealth transfers to trial attorneys associated with class action lawsuits. Moral justice cannot be integrated into the legal establishment when they operate in a war-like mode as King's agents (Rosenbaum 2004).

The partners of Serpente will rotate in and out of government and the regulatory agencies depending on which political party is in power. Their value is enhanced as they have an entrée to the decision makers within the beltway and in the state houses.

The most expensive, prominent law firms provide the three primary legal services to King's company. However, there is a lesser-known role to play for smaller law firms and individual attorneys. Attorneys frequently assume the role of the middlemen in the "pay to play" game. Pay to play happens when a company hires an attorney to provide rather obscure services, and is paid a handsome fee for little or no work. The attorney is the "go-to" person who happens to have remarkable access to the politico who can influence a regulatory or legislative action that would enrich the company. The attorney "opens the door", providing access for the company to the politico. The politico receives personal perks and campaign contributions from the "go-to" attorney. Thus, the attorney launders campaign contributions from the company.

The modus operandi of Serpente is much like that of Ratti. In order to generate the fees from King Rat, they must know what the King wants for himself from the engagement. In "Rainmaking: What all your Junior Lawyers Need to Know" (Compensation

As Banks Bid for City Bond Work, 'Pay to Play' Tradition Endures

Back in 1903, The Wall Street Journal pined for the day "when a man who has built up for himself a large fortune by dishonest trafficking with politicians, for example, in municipal contracts, shall be looked upon as an undesirable member of society." A century later, big municipal-bond "pay to play" cases still arise at a rate of about one a year.

Cites, counties and other entities issue about $400 billion of municipal bonds in the U.S. each year. Banks can earn fees as high as $1 million for underwriting complex deals. While underwriters for some issues are based on low bids, 80% of the deals are "negotiated" ones, in which officials can use other considerations to pick the underwriters. As recently as the early 1990's banks looking for this business frequently, and legally, made campaign donations to municipal officials and other politicians.

But 1994 saw an effort to crack down. A self-regulatory group forbade bond underwriters to do business with municipal officials to whose campaigns they had contributed. The Municipal Securities Rulemaking Board also required disclosure of all contributions by underwriters, and later by consultants as well. The board, whose rules the Securities and Exchange Commission enforces, now is proposing to bar underwriters from using consultants at all when they seek municipal-bond work.

and Benefits for Law Offices 2004), lessons are provided on how to become a superstar in bringing in the clients and the fees. Successful rainmakers know their clients' expectations before beginning work. Clients want a "client-centric" lawyer so that the client can receive the most benefit. Although the corporation is paying the bills, the actual client is the King Rat who is making the decision on what firm to employ. The successful rainmaker will feed the King Rat.

Most law firms have set up canons of ethics that serve to protect their profession from public review and regulation (Mechling 1974). Serpente will proclaim that its services are beyond reproach in upholding the law. These canons of ethics look and sound good; they keep the regulators at bay, and allow Serpente to devour your cheese with impunity.

If you smell a rat, you can be sure that Stinky LLP is not far from the King.

RAT PATROL

Since the outside law firm Stinky LLP operates through Snake, most observers will have little exposure to the partners, such as Serpente. You will also have little exposure to the use of outside attorneys as "go-to" men. These relationships will be kept in a tight circle, to limit fallout if the fraud is uncovered. If Serpente knows one thing, it is how to avoid exposing himself and his partners to prosecutors.

....

Pay to play practices have been tough to root out partly because it can be hard to draw the line between friendly networking and illicit influence-peddling.

Wall Street Journal March 25, 2005

Copyright © 2005 Dow Jones & Company Inc.

CHAPTER 10
Vendor/Contractor—"VC Inc."

Leeches...have a muscular proboscis that allows them to feed on blood drawn from tissues beneath the organism's skin that are well supplied with blood vessels.... Blood feeding leeches usually are equipped with...pouches that allow them to expand considerably during feeding; some leeches consume up to six times their unfed body weight.

Leeches - *Hirudinea*
***Animal Life Encyclopedia*, 2003**

The namesake of the vendors/contractors, the VC, were the communist guerrilla fighters in South Vietnam during the Vietnam War. The VC wore no uniforms; they dressed like the local villagers and blended into the environment. Called "Charlie" by the American Marines, the VC used brutal tactics to intimidate the South Vietnamese into supporting and hiding them. Charlie hid during the day, and came out to fight under the cover of darkness. They burrowed under the ground and formed extensive tunnel systems near Chu Chi, just north of Saigon, to hide from the Americans. These tunnels were too small for the girth of the average American soldier. The Americans had what were called "rat teams", consisting of small-framed Mexican Americans who would enter the tunnels to flush out the VC.

The VC excavated and camouflaged "tiger pits" along trails frequented by American patrols and lined the pit-bottoms with punji sticks--sharpened bamboo coated with excrement. These traps are proudly displayed today in Chu Chi as part of a Disney-like tourist attraction. The VC tortured by putting cages containing rats around the heads of prisoners. "[Rats] show astonishing intelligence in knowing when a human being is helpless" (Orwell 1949, 288). Charlie's savagery included disembowelment of captives and decapitation of opponents. They placed the severed heads on sticks and posted them in villages to maintain control through intimidation. A tour guide in Chu Chi claimed to me that the severed head postings were simply propaganda by the Americans, and never really happened. That's also the story that King would like you to believe about his behavior.

Once the King with the help of Ratti diminishes the internal capabilities of the company, there is need to hire vendors and contractors. Specialty consultants and contractors perform the work formerly done by competent employees who have been discharged.

These VCs operate in the same fashion as their namesake. They operate in a stealth fashion, ambush employees, booby trap paths and torture prisoners.

The VC's are typically FOKers and FOCers who are given the opportunity to siphon dollars out of the firm. They suck the blood out of the company and fill their pouches with your cheese. Similar to the management consultants, they are providing the results that the King demands.

VC consultants are engaged to perform studies that not only are expensive to conduct, but are severely damaging if their recommendations are put into action. In most cases these studies are harmless, because their intention is to simply launder corporate funds by providing consulting contracts to the FOKers and FOCers. Findings are reported to a member of the King's Inner Court, and these findings normally do not see the light of day. For those recommendations that are implemented, the damages to the company are much more severe.

An important prerequisite of becoming a VC is to have club boxes at sporting venues to entertain the King and his Court, as well as their family members. Outings involve lavish expenses at country clubs and hunting lodges. Hunting trips are de rigueur, so that the rats can bag the animal of their choice.

The arrangements between King and Charlie have a formal name--open bi-lateral gratuities (Davia 2000). A gratuity is a favor or a gift given in exchange for a service. Gratuities go astray when they become open bi-lateral gratuities. These are fraudulent exchanges--kickbacks and bribes.

Open bi-lateral gratuities are standard practice in the rat-infested company. In a study reported in the *Wall Street Journal* (Black 1996), 47% of top executives (King Rats), 41% of controllers (Sox) and 76% of graduate business school students (future Rattis) stated that they were willing to commit fraud. These fraudulent activities are principally with vendors and contractors who have similar views of ethical standards.

VCs willing to enter into open bi-lateral gratuities are remarkably successful in securing contracts with the company.

They seem to know what to bid and how to qualify as the successful vendor. Contract rigging gives an intentional advantage to contractors who are FOKers and FOCers.

Charlie is a terrible drain on the company's resources. Since the consulting and contracting fees increase, the need to disembowel more employees becomes inevitable. This usually receives kudos from Wall Street, as the King proclaims that the firm is outsourcing to reduce costs. In a rat infested company, these outsourcing activities erode the core competencies of the firm. Since King and Fats have no regard for the long-term success of the business, this actually works to their benefit. Now they must go to the outside to keep the business running. Remember, unless they go outside, they cannot feed on the benefits that outside firms provide to them. Further, going outside allows them to blame third parties for failure, as they outsource not only the work, but also the responsibility.

VC Inc. creates a serious dilemma for ethical vendors and contractors. If cheating is necessary to get the business, it takes a high degree of integrity to avoid stooping to the level of Charlie. By allowing rat-like behavior to be rewarded, the honest vendor is undermined.

Charlie is sucking the blood from employees whose jobs are outsourced, the honest vendors and contractors who lose business, and the shareholders who end up paying more for an inferior product.

RAT PATROL

VC's are easy to detect, and your knowledge of them will ease your completion of the **DRIAD** test. In the case of consultant FOKers and FOCers, their incompetence normally gives them away to company insiders. For this reason the King will carefully select the company members to work with the consultant. These will be individuals who know little about the subject the consultant is studying, to prevent exposing the ineptitude of the consultant. Since the consultant cannot withstand scrutiny, he or she must be allowed to tear down existing systems with bogus economic analysis and other justifications. Once existing systems are torn down, the consultant can install an inferior and more costly system that will provide a feast of spin-off assignments.

Contractors are also easy to detect. They may get the work through what appear to be bidding procedures, but the key is that they know that they will be allowed to expand the contract through extras, approved by members of the Court. As well, they will be expected to subcontract with FOKers and FOCers for the provision of supplies and services. Look for the King Rat's brother on the payroll of the winning bidder.

The most accurate way to identify VCs is for the Rat Patrol to examine the flight manifest and destination of King's corporate jet, guests at the company hunting or fishing lodge, and members of his foursome. Since King usually wins the prize giveaways at such outings, a strong correlation exists with the number of shotguns, hunting jackets, golf shirts, dozens of golf balls and miscellaneous logo-embossed freebees stashed in King's home. Of course, this method of detection is only available if you have access to his wardrobe closet.

CHAPTER 11

Investment Banker—
"I.B. Churns & U.R. Burned"

Their habit of collecting objects is not unusual, as rodents are well-known thieves. Where the wood rat differs is that it often appears to "pay" for what it takes by leaving some other object in its place. What actually happens is that the wood rat collects one item, and is in the process of carrying it home when it finds something better, so it drops its original prize in favor of the more desirable one.

Desert Wood Rat--*Neotoma lepida*
***World of Animals*, 2003**

The most glamorous rat is considered to be the Black and White Maned Rat of Africa (*Lophiomyinae*). When irritated, this beautiful rat raises its hair like a porcupine to frighten its enemies (Henderickson 1983). So too are the investment banker rats, dressed to perfection with their custom suits, bright suspenders, crisply starched white-collared blue-striped shirts, and gold cuff links. Or, in today's world, dressed in their designer suits, silk blouses, gold bracelets and Jimmy Choos. They are clearly the most beautiful rats in the King's Court. The investment bankers we will discuss belong to the white-paw firm of I.B. Churns & U.R. Burned, better known as Churn & Burn, or simply Churn.

The financial crisis of 2008-09 nearly has eliminated the large, stand-alone investment banking firm. However, the services that they provided, at astronomical costs, will continue. The financial meltdown is the "ultimate churn and burn".

Only top MBAs from elite business schools and from the proper rat species are allowed to join the most prestigious firms such as Churn & Burn. The firm specializes in serving corporations with banking, merger and acquisition, brokerage and research services. Its goal is to achieve lucrative fee generating business by lending the name of the firm to any transaction. If you hire Churn & Burn, King and Fats are immunized from challenge for their poor decisions.

Churn & Burn's fees bear no resemblance to their services. Despite resembling the Black and White Maned Rat, many of its partners uncannily exhibit the behavior of the Wood Rat: stealing and then carrying their reward back to the burrow for consumption. They especially like shiny objects, such as gold and jewels. The partners of Churn & Burn have an excellent nose for maximizing fees. They know that if they find a King Rat, they have found a treasure trove of precious metals and jewels.

Churn's partners always travel with several junior Churns to carry their Fuller Brush Man-sized bags, holding multiple copies of the glossy booklets explaining the capabilities of Churn & Burn. They typically have a pack of four or five rats on any engagement. Their goal is to convince King to make changes in the asset portfolio or the financial structure of his company. They want to double or triple dip into your cheese.

First they want the merger and acquisition fees when they convince King to buy another company or to sell a portion of his company. Next they want the financing fees. These fees keep on giving because they represent annual business rather than a one-shot treasure trove. Once the deal is consummated, Churn will

Price to Pay for Knowing too Much

"I can't predict my demise, but I suspect it will come abruptly." Thus foretold Ivan "The Terrible" Boesky a short time before he was unmasked as Wall Street's biggest crook.

As so often, he was already ahead of the game. For six months, Boesky had been wearing a bug to help to finger other members of an insider-trading ring that amassed a fortune betting on US takeovers.

Boesky, whose "greed is healthy" speech inspired the Hollywood character Gordon Gekko, made more than $200 million. His web of tipsters extended from big-hitting bankers, lawyers and accountants to airport check-in clerks and chauffeurs, who would tip him the wink when company chiefs secretly met rivals.

Boesky's nemesis was Rudy Giuliani, a promising young lawyer in the New York District Attorney's office determined to clean up Wall Street.

Giuliani, later Mayor of New York, forced Boesky to sing like a canary, revealing, among other things, an illegal share support operation that helped Guinness to use its frothy paper to buy Distillers in 1986. Because of Boesky's testimony, Ernest Saunders, the Guinness chairman, Gerald Ronson, the property magnate, and Anthony Parnes, the stockbroker, served time in prison.

Boesky's plea-bargaining also felled Michael Milken, architect of the high risk "junk bond" market, and prompted the collapse of his Drexel Burnham Lambert, one of the most aggressive investment banks on Wall Street. Boesky, who was born in 1937, served two years in a California prison, where he tended the flower beds.

Times of London November 14, 2005
Copyright © 2005 NI Syndication Ltd.

help restructure King's company to accommodate the new assets. They will run the interference for King with his board (as if that's a problem) and with the shareholders. Invariably, they run their economic models to show that the company is paying or receiving fair value for its acquisitions or dispositions. Its financial modeling will show how the stock price will increase once this brilliant deal is consummated. Churn will bring in its Stinky LLP to perform legal due diligence on the target company.

Soon after the deal is done Churn & Burn's research arm will prepare a glowing report of King's management and deal making abilities. With the short-term stock price increasing, with a little help from other investment banks, Churn & Burn now has an open door to King for an endless stream of fees.

These are rich deals for the investment bankers. Hence, the payday for a Churn partner in a good year is between $5 and $15 million. Where does this money come from? Churn's partners would say that it's from economic efficiency, and that the firm is creating value for the shareholder. Indeed, Churn's analysis shows the cost savings from the merger or acquisition. After the merger, you lose your job so

CEO Pay Takes a Hit in Bailout Plan

Perhaps nowhere has excessive pay been more pervasive than at many of the financial firms now foundering. David DeBoskey, a San Diego State University professor, estimates American International Group, Fannie Mae and Freddie Mac... paid their top executives a total of $1.4 billion in salaries, bonuses and stock-related pay from 2003 to 2007. Last year alone, top executives at Wall Street investment banks Goldman Sachs, Merrill Lynch, Morgan Stanley, Bear Stearns and Lehman received a combined $613 million, or an average of $123 million at each firm, says pay expert Graef Crystal, author of *The Crystal Report on Executive Compensation.*

USA Today September 29, 2008
© 2008 USA Today, a division of Gannett Co.

---

that King can demonstrate the cost savings. When performance wanes, Churn will return to unwind the deal that caused the trouble, and once again reap fantastic rewards. The greatest rewards of the sub-prime mortgage debacle are yet to come!

When working for a King Rat, Churn's job is well understood. It is to feed the King and to protect the King and the board from shareholder lawsuits. The most prominent investment banks are routinely charged with malfeasance, but that does not seem to affect their reputation. When the firm is caught in a fraudulent act, it receives a slap on the wrist, some middle-level banker may go to jail, and the firm's penalty is peanuts compared to the amount stolen.

In *Den of Thieves*, Stewart (1991) stated that Wall Street criminals are the consummate evaluators of risk. In addition, Stewart contends that the code of silence among the investment banks allows crimes to occur repeatedly within the most respected institutions. The fees generated by illicit behavior are so large, and the penalties for getting caught so small, that the game is well worth playing. If caught, they can afford the most powerful lawyers and public relations firms to defend their actions. Their attorneys accuse the government prosecutors of overreaching. Churn will call in its chits from the politicos to have them call off the dogs. This is simply quid pro quo for the campaign contributions and the other miscellaneous funds that end up in the pockets of the politicos.

Whenever the King Rat is to gain from a transaction (which is always the case, or the deal would not advance), shareholders beware. Management buyouts of shareholders are particularly incestuous. The King has the ability to control the flow of information and establish the value to suit himself and his board (Bruner and Paine 1988). Management and its bankers become fabulously wealthy from buying out a company at a discounted price, and then flipping the company through an initial public offering or sale to a private equity firm.

One of the best features of Churn & Burn is that they have better seats at sporting events than the run-of-the-mill VC. With their sponsorship of major sporting events, King, Fats and Sox are invited to the US Open Tennis Tournament, the Masters, the Super Bowl and the World Series. How else can a rat get to play golf with a PGA tour leader and have his family rub shoulders with movie stars in the hospitality tent? But this is just a side dish from the investment bankers.

The real meal for King is the golden handshake given once a deal is consummated in which the King's services are no longer needed. How about $10 to $20 million for selling out his employees and shareholders. Not a bad chunk of cheese.

Churning is the best way to make cheese for the King and his Court. It all starts with cream. The cream is your job, the inherent value of your shares as a stockholder, and your benefits as a retiree. With government bailouts as the new trend, you will also "be creamed" by paying higher taxes and by having less purchasing power due to a devalued dollar. The investment bankers will churn the cream and turn it into cheese. They will feast on the cheese along with King and his Court, feeling no remorse for the destruction that they have left in their path.

RAT PATROL

The presence of Churn is detected by frequent employment of investment bankers to buy and sell assets or businesses, and with costly, exotic financing schemes. If the deal structure is complicated with multiple corporations, offshore entities, private partnerships and exotic financing, you can be sure that Churn is lurking nearby. The exotic derivatives that have become front page headlines (such as credit default option swaps, CDOS) are prime (or should I say sub-prime) warning signs.

In addition, Churn's presence is highly correlated with the presence of King Rat and Fats at the Masters, PGA, US Open and British Open golf tournaments; the Grand Slam of tennis; the NCAA basketball tournament; the college bowl games, the Super Bowl; and the World Series. The Rat Patrol can identify through the rumor mill the presence of the King and selected members of his Court at such premier events.

By identifying high level government officials hired into Churn's firm after retiring from "public service"; by adding up the campaign contributions, inauguration party contributions and hosted-political fundraisers by Churn's partners; and by discovering Churn's contributions to King's favorite charity, you will be able to justify an increase in the **DRIAD**.

CHAPTER 12
Wall Street Analyst—"Wimpy MBA"

You're a mouse studying to be a rat.

Wilson Mizner
Playwright
1876-1933

he Wall Street analysts are distinctive in the rat pack since they appear much younger than the other rats-- almost mouse-like. They are cute and cuddly. Their whiskers have not yet emerged. Whenever in the presence of the King or Spin, they are milquetoast.

Wimpy MBA is typical of the analysts. He or she often is a member of the investment banking firm I.B. Churns & U.R. Burned. Wimp is responsible for valuing King Rat's company, and evaluating the effectiveness of management. This may seem to be fraught with conflicts with the investment banking arm of the business, but we are assured that there is a "Chinese wall" separating the analyst from the banking side. However, this wall has been built with Swiss cheese. It is your cheese, and it has holes so big that any claim of independence does not meet the laugh test.

In addition to youth, Wimp appears to be terribly naïve to the casual observer. This is because Wimp brings his/her spreadsheet to Spin's office, and gets Spin to fill in all the numbers. Unlike Ratti, whose chief communication device is PowerPoint, Wimp works in Excel. Amazingly, Wimp comes up with the same earnings projections that King and Sox have decided meet their current interests.

Wimpy's real responsibilities are to help win investment banking business for his employer, and to move the price of the stock. He or she is young, but has been trained by senior analysts who have been feeding for decades. The goal is investment banking and financing revenues generated on the other side of the Chinese wall. If Wimp does not play the game, then his or her firm is shut out of the investment banking business, and he or she moves on to another firm. Wimp usually recommends a stock after it goes up and then says it will go higher. However, sometimes King wants the stock to go down because his friends have moved to short positions. Then he feeds low forecasts to Wimp to drive the stock down.

In *Searching for the Corporate Savior,* Harvard Business School Professor Rakesh Khurana (2002) observed that the Wall Street analysts have contributed to the increased focus on the CEO. The CEO has increasingly become an intermediary between the investors and the firm, and the CEO affects the short-term price movement of the stock.

If Wimpy does his or her job well, all members of the Court are elated: The King is glorified in the analyst reports; Wimp keeps a job; the stock goes up and down at the right time; Wimp's company gets the investment banking business; the

FOKers and FOCers make a killing on the stock; and the trading volume is high so the traders on the floor (also from Wimp's company) increase their take.

The only losers in the game are the shareholders who believe that the game is honest. Those short-term traders who believe that Wimp's analysis is credible lose their shirts. Long-term investors also lose as King erodes shareholder value over time.   The excesses of the 1990's have been written about extensively. Sell ratings accounted for less than 2% of analysts' recommendations (Vickers et al 2002). Enron paid $323 million to Wall Street in underwriting fees from 1986 to 1992 (ibid.). None of this wrongdoing seemed to have any impact on the firms or their industry.

Dobson (2003) attributes the failings of finance professionals to acculturation--the implicit education into a certain moral value system. Individuals become acculturated by the day-to-day behavior, and that behavior is assumed to be normal. "Honest behavior would be considered deviant and place the firm at a disadvantage" (ibid.,32).

If Wimpy MBA does not act like a rat, his or her behavior is irrational and deviant.

RAT PATROL

You should have members on your Rat Patrol that have extensive knowledge of your company's business and the industry in which it operates. These individuals should read carefully the reports prepared by Wimpy. If a report is filled with boilerplate, repetition, trivia and little true understanding of the drivers of the business, it most likely was written by Wimpy. If they find themselves smirking or outright laughing when reading a report, you can be sure that the author is a Wimp!

CHAPTER 13

Hedge Funds, Mutual Funds and Private Equity Firms—"Hedgy, Mute & Privy"

[Hedge Funds] are numerous and loaded with cash. Rarely loners, they hunt in packs....

Hedge Funds: The New Raiders
Business Week, 2005

edgy, Mute & Privy represent the hedge funds, mutual funds and private equity firms that dominate trading in the shares of King's company. Mute has been influential for many years, Privy has been gaining strength, and Hedgy has shown incredible proliferation in financial markets.

Hedgy, in particular, is the type of owner that King and Fats have always dreamed about. Hedgy is not a long-term investor looking for value growth. Rather, Hedgy is looking for rapid movements of the stock--up or down. Hedgy loves volatility. He doesn't really care which way the stock moves--as long as it moves in the direction of his bet. In fact, Hedgy works in concert with other rats of like kind to move the market in the direction of their choice. Hedgy is one of the most aggressive rats in the kingdom, and he is one of the least regulated, allowing exceptional latitude for covert operations.

Hedgy is a Kangaroo Rat. Known for fighting ability, the Kangaroo Rat has large cheek pouches for storing food. He is a small rat with a large head, large black eyes and rounded ears and a long tail. Its head is almost the size of his body (Morris and Beer 2003). The rat forages at night, carrying its food in its cheek pouches to deposit in burrow storerooms, usually located in the backcountry of Greenwich, Connecticut. The Kangaroo Rat neither pants nor sweats. A fearless rat, he often prefers stealing from others rather than gathering his own food (Gilbreath 1979).

Hedgy trades based upon headlines in the newspaper. In fact, Hedgy usually knows the headline before it is printed. Thus, when the average investor acts on the news, Hedgy has already locked in his profits from his seemingly all-knowing intuition.

Hedgy, and his close relatives Mute and Privy, are getting inside information. Never mind Regulation FD. This regulation was supposed to protect the shareholder from unequal information. What it does in reality is provide cover for King, Fats and Spin. They can appear to follow strict guidelines, but you are not with them 24 hours a day. Under cover of darkness, the signals are sent so that Hedgy, Mute & Privy are advantaged. Call it country club talk, conversation over dinner, or other social banter, inside information will be leaked. If he holds enough stock, Fats will nominate Mute's or Hedgy's second cousin to the company's board to ensure regular inside information flow. In return, King and Fats will be afforded investment opportunities not available to the average investor.

A study by Professor Stefan Nagel reported in Stanford Business (2005) showed that hedge funds confounded the efficient market theorists in the tech bubble of 1998 to 2000. During the tech bubble, hedge funds rode up the market and then backed out just before the market fell. "If you can predict what the irrational guys are doing, then it may be entirely rational to buy irrationally-priced stocks," said Nagel (p. 26).

Top hedge fund managers collected windfall fees in 2007

The top hedge fund managers took home dizzying sums last year, fed by a bull market in commodities and investors' willingness to pay up for proven track records.

Institutional Investor's Alpha reported Wednesday the top 50 hedge fund managers earned a combined $29 billion in 2007. Five managers earned more than $1 billion.

One contributor to the enormous amounts of money hedge fund managers are making is the unraveling of the traditional "2 and 20" method of compensation. For years, funds typically charged 2 percent of the amount invested plus 20 percent of the profits.

Ezra Zask of Lakeville Capital Management, a hedge fund advisory, said some of the bigger hedge funds are now charging as much as 5 percent of the invested principal and 40 percent of the profits.

....

Driven in part by fees hedge fund managers are making, income inequality in 2007 was at the highest level since 1928, the year before the Great Depression began.

International Herald Tribune April 16, 2008
Copyright © 2008 The Associated Press

[Author's Note: Perhaps income inequality is a good leading indicator for financial depressions.]

There are over 7000 hedge funds, about the same as the number of mutual funds (Economist 2005a). Hedge funds account for half of the daily volume on the New York Stock Exchange (ibid.). They operate under an exemption from the 1940 Investment Act that defines mutual funds. The secretive nature of the funds makes them prime vehicles for abuse. Typically 20% to 30% of trading profit goes to the hedge fund manager plus an annual management fee of 1% to 2%. Hedge funds can be incredibly profitable to the manager if he is able to predict the short-term movement of a stock. Whenever billions of dollars are at stake, depending on the direction of a bet, the rats will swarm to the person who holds the key to the pantry.

The hedge fund manager is the new Wall Street elite. No wonder housing prices have skyrocketed on Nantucket, and private jets line the tarmac at Westchester County Airport, only a five minute drive from Hedgy's Greenwich estate.

Despite the failure rate of hedge funds in the 2008 financial crisis, Hedgy's personal assets are secure, as he has invested his windfall outside of the hedge fund. His personal portfolio is stashed away in government-guaranteed investments. In this manner, his life-style is not interrupted by the financial meltdown caused by excessive leverage and financial derivatives.

A Dangerous Game:

Hedge funds have gotten rich from credit derivatives. Will they blow up?

...[I]f you want to fret over the next financial catastrophes, turn your gaze away from energy futures and focus on something far more obscure: credit default swaps. Hedge funds are neck-deep in these derivatives, and if something goes wrong, the pain will be widespread.

....

Hedge funds account for 58% of the trading in these derivatives, says Greenwich Associates, a financial research firm. Selling protection has been a big moneymaker for funds like $23 billion (assets) D.E. Shaw and $12 billion Citadel, say market participants, and for specialized outfits like Primus Guaranty in Bermuda, which took in $57 million in the first half of 2006 selling protection on $1.6 billion in debt.

With corporate debt defaults low these days, the temptation is high to write insurance policies on bonds. A hedge fund can make $60,000 to $1 million a year selling protection on $10 million in bonds. It's like finding money in the street. Unless, of course, the economy suddenly enters a recession. If that happens, hedge funds addicted to the credit market will be in deep trouble. "A lot of [hedge funds] have sold insurance, are sitting on the premiums--and are bare-ass," says Charles Gradante, cofounder of Hennessee Group, which tracks hedge fund performance. "If there is a Long Term Capital-type systemic risk potential out there, it's in the [credit swap] market."

The size of the hedge fund industry is one-sixth of mutual funds, but is providing more revenue. Hedge funds conduct business through a prime broker who extracts fees through stock and bond lending charges and trading fees. Investment banks collect about $15 billion annually from hedge funds, producing $6 billion in profits (Economist 2005a). Churn does not want to see its profits from hedge funds erode, since this fee-based income is as good as printing money. No risk and guaranteed profits to administer Hedgy's business is a great way to make a living.

Warren Buffett (2006) has a name for Hedgy and Privy-- he calls them "Hyper-Helpers." "Manager-Helpers" is the moniker that Buffett put on brokers (Wimpy), fund managers (Mute) and consultants (Ratti, Churn and Charlie), all of whom erode your return on investment by taking enormous fees. Hyper-Helpers take an even greater share of your cheese. "Hyper-Helpers are really just Manager-Helpers wearing new uniforms, bearing sewn-on sexy names like HEDGE FUND or PRIVATE EQUITY" (ibid.,17).

Turning to the mutual fund industry, from 1990 to 2002 mutual fund assets increased from $1 trillion to $7 trillion in 8,900 mutual funds (Economist 2003). Mute and other top managers of mutual funds make over $20 million per year. Such funds account for 23% of publicly traded stock (ibid.).

Mutual fund operating costs exceed $123 billion (ibid.). These may be costs to the funds, but much of the "cost" is income to those managing the funds. These costs include management fees, administrative fees, custodian and transfer fees, legal and audit fees, interest costs and 112b-1 fees. All of these "costs" are revenues to the likes of Churn & Burn, Stinky LLP and the others that are skimming from your mutual fund gains.

You would think that Mute and friends would be satisfied with $20 million per year. But no, when a rat feeds as easily as

....

The credit-derivatives business is dominated by 14 dealers. Among them: JPMorgan Chase, Citigroup, Bank of America, Goldman Sachs and Morgan Stanley. All have staggering amounts of derivatives on their books: JPMorgan's notional exposure was $3.6 trillion as of June 30, according to the Federal Deposit Insurance Corp., which is almost three times assets and 30 times capital. Credit derivatives at Wachovia Corp. have jumped sevenfold since 2003 to $170 billion, more than three times capital. Banks love derivatives because they provide multiple ways to make money. Revenue from all types of derivatives will hit $34 billion or so this year at U.S. banks and securities firms, says Tower Group, a financial-research outfit, with hedge funds generating much of the money.

....

Regulators say there's no reason to worry--yet. All big banks require hedge funds to back up their swaps with cash collateral that is adjusted daily, says Kathryn Dick, deputy comptroller for credit and market risk at the Office of the Comptroller of the Currency.

Forbes.com October 16, 2006
© 2006 Forbes
[Author's Note: R.I.P. exactly two years later. Daniel Fisher, Senior Editor of Forbes magazine, was "spot-on" making this call back in October 2006.]

Mute, he wants more and more. In addition to fees, they have been cited for late trading and market timing abuses costing investors billions annually.

Convictions for insider trading abuses are difficult to obtain, even for the worst offenders. This gives comfort to the rats that the chances of being caught are minimal. The idea is to have a sufficient gray area where lawbreakers can hide... "lawyers, investment bankers, proxy solicitors, PR men, printers and confidants are too preoccupied with making money to be concerned with ethics or fair play in the markets on which they base their livelihood" (Stevens 1987, 256).

Privy's primary game is to buy out companies, drain them of cash and then let them flounder. Standard and Poors' reports that dividend recapitalizations by private equity firms have exceeded $50 billion in the previous two years (Sender 2006). The key to Privy's success is to make sure that it can take more money out of their portfolio of companies than they have put in. With easy financing from Churn & Burn, they load these companies with debt and take out the cash for themselves. Also, they charge high management fees to the companies that they have bought.

No wonder when markets are soft these companies cannot make their debt payments, and management must cut pensions and benefits to prevent bankruptcy. Privy flushes your retiree pension and healthcare benefits down the toilet. He and his investors have the cash that was intended to pay for your benefits. If the company fails and falls into bankruptcy, he walks away a winner. The banks that loaned Privy the money will stand in front of you in the debtors' line, and the federal taxpayer will pick up the pension bill under the PBGC.

The serious, negative impact of stock ownership by institutions has not been fully recognized. Institutional ownership does not care about long-term value growth of a company. They care about short-term stock movements. Elmer Johnson (1990) in his lecture "Ethics and Corporate Governance in the Age of

Takeover Artists Quench Thirst
Many Private-Equity Firms Drain Out Dividends and Fees, Saddling Companies With Debt.

In a technique practically unheard of just five years ago, private-equity firms, emboldened by easy financing, are paying themselves lavish dividends and fees from companies they acquire. Typically, private-equity firms have generated returns by acquiring companies with a mix of cash and debt, taking them private, restructuring them, and then either taking them public or selling them.

But a favorable financing environment has given rise to a high volume of dividends and fees, often paid well ahead of any operational turnaround, primarily through aggressive issuance of debt by the acquired companies...

In the past two years, private-equity firms garnered more than $50 billion from so-called dividend recapitalizations, according to Standard & Poor's Corp. By contrast, there were virtually no such dividend financings just five years ago. As much as 50% of the returns that buyout firms have paid their investors in the past two years came from such dividends, financed mostly with new debt, according to calculations by some private-equity firms.

....

Some worry that by heaping enormous debt onto their portfolio companies to help pay the dividends, private-equity firms heighten the risk that the companies may fail if the economy stumbles. Should it "be about how far you can push things or

Pension Fund Capitalism" remarked that institutions have no intention of monitoring management. They prefer the power of exit rather than trying to change management, and they vote with their feet rather than their voice. Given that they trade frequently, there is no interest in long-term decisions. This short-term focus is a disease that quickly spreads to management, according to Johnson.

Rat infested managements who are playing to the institutions don't give a rat's tail about long-term decisions. Management will talk about long-term goals, but when it comes to putting up the money, you won't see spending for research and development or for projects that will not yield immediate returns. That would be three CEOs in the future! Propaganda issued by Spin is sufficient to mislead the individual investor who is interested in ownership responsibility.

Massive transfers of wealth (your cheese) are occurring in the activities of the hedge funds, mutual funds and private equity firms. Where else can you earn $5 to $20 million per year if you can't hit like A-Rod? The potential to become the next Hedgy, Mute or Privy is drawing many of the brightest (but certainly not the best) of our graduates. If you and coming Rat, why be a doctor, are an up a scientist

should it be about how much flexibility you give your companies to deal with the unexpected?" asks Josh Lerner, a professor at Harvard Business School, who has done research on the performance of private-equity firms. " You can see reason to worry in how much [money] they are pulling out."

Wall Street Journal January 5, 2006
Copyright © 2006 Dow Jones & Company Inc.

or an engineer--and limit your income potential. Rats move to the place where the cheese is piled the highest--and even today, that pile is in the financial community (despite the meltdown).

RAT PATROL

You will never be able to detect Hedgy, Mute and Privy--so don't bother to waste the time of the Rat Patrol. The only way that you may be able to detect them is to have a GPS ankle bracelet on the King Rat, and find out how much time he spends in Greenwich, Connecticut. After all, the Securities and Exchange Commission couldn't detect Bernie Madoff.

CHAPTER 14
Executive Search Firm—"H. Hunter Gmb"

The external CEO labor "market" operates as a circulation of elites within a single, sealed-off system relying on socially legitimated criteria that--contrary to conventional economic wisdom--are not to be confused with relevant skills for the CEO position.... Most corporate directors are CEOs themselves, and thus the direct beneficiaries of a way of thinking that creates an artificial scarcity of "talent" and thereby justifies paying CEOs with boundless extravagance.

Professor Rakesh Khurana
Harvard Business School
Searching for the Corporate Savior, **2002**

ing and Fats will go to extraordinary lengths to prevent new competitors into the game. By limiting the field of competition, there is more cheese to go around for the privileged few (especially themselves). This is where the executive search firm, H. Hunter Gmb, becomes a very important member of the team. H. Hunter not only aids and abets the stealing of your cheese, but is an important player in perpetuating the process.

In a rat infested company, the board of directors rarely wants to promote an insider to the CEO position. Professor Khurana (2002) observed the growing tendency for boards to appoint outside candidates to the CEO position rather than to promote from within the company. The playing field is tilted toward the outside candidate because this outcome increases the feeding of board members and the executive search firm.

The essential function of the executive search firm is to "facilitate the social dimensions of the external CEO search process while simultaneously helping to disguise them—thus helping the search to achieve legitimacy in the eyes of interested observers" (ibid.,xv). Khurana wryly observes, "the selection of a new CEO [is] a process sometimes described as only slightly less mysterious than the election of a new pope" (ibid.,x).

Thus, the role of H. Hunter is to provide legitimacy where there is none. Hunter will be highly paid to provide cover for the board and to restrict competition for the CEO slot to social contacts of the board members. Closing off the process to genuine competition is the key role of Hunter--to prevent the rat pack from becoming too crowded, thus diluting the take and preventing someone with true competence to compete for the job.

Remember, the board rats are thinking of maximizing their own cheese in the selection of the CEO. If you are a qualified insider in a rat infested company, the prospects of your elevation to the CEO position are nil. Going outside the company allows the board rats to (1) display creativity, (2) blame others (namely Hunter) for the selection of the CEO in the event of failure (which is highly probable), and (3) increase their own chances for other board and CEO appointments. Success of the corporation is irrelevant to the decision. Rat infested companies don't invest in developing insiders to become managers because there is no reward for doing this. They are rewarded by churning CEOs and having a legitimate scapegoat. In the anti-rat book *Good to Great*, Jim Collins (2001) found that the best run organizations had CEOs without marquee value, and that exceptional companies recruited internally.

Selection of an outsider shows that the board is an instrument of change. Since the board knows insiders better than outsiders, promotion of the insider is riskier for the board (Khurana 2002). Fats and the other board rats would subject themselves to criticism that their internal selection, whom they should know well, was not up to the job. In addition, an insider knows the company and the industry better than the board members, resulting in a loss of power for the board. Board

members cannot reward their social acquaintances if an insider is selected.

Looking from the perspective of H. Hunter, the search fee is maximized if an outsider is brought in--typically this amounts to about one-third of first year compensation (Economist 2002b). Hunter increases its potential for repeat business since it takes responsibility for the new hire and takes the heat off the board. The game is biased against finding the best person for the job. It is also biased toward a high turnover rate. When the board fires a CEO (and pays him off to leave quietly) the stock price will increase showing a proactive board. The search firm increases its income with another search. The board has another opportunity to pad the wallet of another friend.

The new King will have the same attributes as the old King because recycling keeps the fees flowing. As for the board members and the old King Rat, Hunter will reward them with outstanding recommendations for other board and CEO positions.

Hunter will go through what appears to be an exhaustive search. However, what really happens is that Hunter asks the board for a list of candidates (and then may add one or two additional names of rats that have played their game in the past). The names on the list are invariably friends of Fats and the other board rats. Fats and Hunter will throw in a couple of insiders and perhaps a couple of legitimate outsiders who are capable of doing the job. When the short list is formed this sense of legitimacy will be retained. But when the final decision is made--the answer is the one that Fats wanted in the beginning. Hunter is throwing a masquerade party and everyone knows it. However, by having the appointment go through such an apparently rigorous process, the board is protected. Hunter is simply providing cover for a price. And the price is high.

The net upshot is that you may have been on the short list, but you just missed out on the promotion. You get to report to a rat with the same qualities as Old King and Fats. This means that you will have to do all of the work, but get none of the credit. Fats is happy because the board has a new King Rat. Old King is happy because he receives a golden handshake, and Hunter will find a new position for him elsewhere. Hunter is happy because he has maximized his fees, and he has cemented his relationship with New King and Fats assuring the next engagement.

The process just described maximizes the compensation for the King and Court, and ensures that the best persons are excluded from receiving the job. This increases the turnover of CEOs--which of course is the dream of Hunter. More turnover equates to more fees. The last thing wanted is stability. What is desired is the stealing (oops, movement) of cheese!

Why is an executive search firm necessary to find suitable candidates? The fact that no suitable internal candidates have been developed is a clear sign of failure of the management and the board. However, in retrospect, this should not be surprising in a rat infested company.

The selection process is over before it begins. The board knows who will be the CEO. Khurana (2002) compared the executive search firm's role to that of a master of ceremonies, rather than an honest broker facilitating communications between candidates and the board. Fats and his fellow board rats believe that Bert Parks would make an excellent H. Hunter.

A new King Rat is often selected for star power or as a marquee rat.   Seventy-five percent of outsiders appointed to CEO positions had previously been CEOs or presidents of other companies (Economist 2006). King must be able to play to Wall Street and move the stock price. In today's world of institutional ownership of stock, the main task of King is to work with Wimpy, Hedgy, Mute and Privy. In this way they can recommend the stock and buy at the right time (as well as downgrade and sell at the right time). The question is not long-term value, but how the stock will move in the short run. Running a company to increase value is hard work--the last thing on the mind of a King Rat.

By bringing in an outsider, the board has an opportunity to ratchet up the compensation of the CEO. An external candidate can bargain for his compensation package, whereas this is difficult for an insider being promoted. The board can justify paying an "above average" salary to get an "above average" performer. This ties in nicely with the outside HR consulting firm's role in bidding up salaries and bonuses.

In exchange for an above average compensation package, New King will be sure to justify an increase in the board's compensation. This, of course, will be legitimatized by another consultant's study. The entire process is extremely costly, not only the payments to the consultants, but also in the increasing remuneration of executives and board members. But after all, this gluttony is the objective of the rats, and that is why the rats are so successful in defending their turf. The stakes get higher and higher, and the game has the outward appearance of legitimacy.

Hunter protects the board from any appearance of impropriety and limits the risk of criticism. This is why Hunter is compensated so well, and why, when Fats hires Hunter, he will get one of the big names in the field. How can you criticize a selection that was vetted by one of the largest, most successful, search firms in the world?

We end this chapter where we started. The goal is to limit the number of rats that are feeding by those already at the trough. Experimental studies on Brown rats showed that they "reached states of highly injurious aggressive behavior as populations become crowded and social disintegration occurred" (Southwick 1970,6). Rats do not want open markets for their positions. "The supreme irony [is] that--to the extent that capitalism is a system based on openness and competition--corporate directors, when they come to choose a new CEO, can be some of the fiercest opponents of capitalism anywhere." These words by Professor Khurana (2002,218) express the rat-like behavior precisely.

The feeding frenzy of the rats continues. If you thought that you would be promoted on merit, forget about it. You are needed to do the work. When your worth has been extracted, you will become expendable. In other words, your cheese will be moved. Hunter is a critical member of the King's Outer Court.

RAT PATROL

The use of an executive search firm to find a new King Rat or members of the Court is a tip-off to the Patrol that rats may be present. The issue is how King and Fats use the firm. Much like the use of other consultants, there may be a legitimate need to employ an outside search firm. In such cases, the scope of the search firm is carefully established to provide support, rather than cover. If it appears that King and Fats are using the firm as a master of ceremonies, then you have reason to increase the **DRIAD**.

A lesser-known, insidious role for search firms is the management assessment assignment. This is where Hunter reviews the qualifications of current managers for promotion. This is a clear sign of a King Rat. First, if he and his board members don't know the qualifications of key executives in the company, they are derelict in their duty to begin with. Secondly, whatever the assessment reveals, the results are first presented privately to King and Fats. The assessor is sufficiently savvy to know what the answer is supposed to be before he submits his formal report. In this role, Hunter is working as an assassin on behalf of King and Fats.

CHAPTER 15

External Auditor—"Green I. Shade LLP"

Wild rats thus possess a delicately balanced and highly efficient combination of movements of approach and avoidance, which enables them safely to make the most of what the environment has to offer.

The Rat: A Study in Behaviour, 1963

reen I. Shade LLP has been in the *Wall Street Journal* frequently for failure to properly audit fraudulent behavior by King's company. In the past Shady enjoyed the feast from conflicts of interest resulting from the consulting arm of this limited liability partnership. In this role, Shady provided ammunition for King to circumvent paying taxes and reporting meaningful financial results. Since Shady was also the external auditor, it knew precisely how to skirt the regulations to meet the letter, but not the spirit of the law. Whether King needed convoluted financial structures to keep debt off the balance sheet, recommendations for tax evasion that were purported to be "tax efficiency," or ways around the internal and external accounting control structures, Shady's advice was available for a price. When Shady's partners put on their green eyeshades as external auditor, they were certain to declare no responsibility for catching fraudulent behavior in the company. Ray Garrett former Chairman of the Securities and Exchange Commission has said, "A really successful fraud can scarcely be accomplished in our complex financial world without the help of accountants and lawyers" (Mechling 1974).

Most observers of the current regulatory environment related to accounting and financial reporting would assume that corporate rats would have a difficult time committing fraud. The common perception is that corporate executives committing fraud will be caught by the tightening control structures and greater board oversight. This perception is reinforced by the significant number of prominent executives who are caught red-handed.

Wrong again! What is reported in the *Wall Street Journal* is the tip of the iceberg. In *Fraud 101: Techniques and Strategies for Detection*, Howard Davia (2000) lists three types of fraud:

- Group 1--Exposed to the public domain.

- Group 2--Discovered by entities, but the details are not made public.

- Group 3--Not detected, known only to the perpetrators.

Fraud in most rat infested companies falls into Groups 2 and 3--fraud that you will never hear about in the newspapers. Groups 2 and 3 are estimated to represent 80 percent of all fraud! (ibid.). Fraud that you don't see, that is conducted underground and under the cover of darkness, is the type of fraud being perpetrated by King Rats. This is the fraud that is not caught (or at least not made public), as rats know how to avoid the poison. Davia calls Group 2 and 3 frauds the "hard core" that remains after the greedy and inept are discovered.

The public believes that Group 1 fraud is typical of all fraud--that those committing fraud are caught and brought to justice. Davia points out that the Groups 2 and 3 frauds are committed by the cunning and conservative perpetrators who do not make

Academia: Audit Committees May Be Key to Restoring Confidence

As unfolding accounting scandals at WorldCom, Adelphia and Xerox rock a profession still reeling from the effects of the Enron/Andersen mess, academics suggested a number of measures to restore the profession's credibility in the eyes of the public.

The events of the past eight months, compounded with those still unfolding, haven't done much to restore the profession's tarnished reputation. As investors wonder whether the financial statements of multi-billion dollar companies are worth the paper they're printed on and regulators and Congressional representatives question the accounting profession's ability to police itself, members of the academic community offered advice on how to help restore public confidence.

"We need to get the audit committee in charge of dealing with the auditor instead of dealing with the CFO's office," said Roman Weil, an accounting professor at the University of Chicago. "Who picks the auditor right now? Management. The audit committee is supposed to have that power, but they haven't been behaving that way. To make the auditor credible, you have to have the audit committee play the role it's supposed to play. CFOs have gotten to the position where they say, 'show me where it says I can't do this. If you can't, then I'm going to do it.'"

Accounting Today July 22, 2002
Copyright 2002 by Source Media

mistakes leading to familiar, it is--this is the them so difficult to

Davia also controls are usually to detecting fraud-- two or more individuals the fraud. Therefore, in the King and his Court, be detected by Shady.

"Independent" auditing the financial by Sox for King's have their fees One might say that really working under audit committee of independently with without King and Sox independence is more Fats has carefully chosen to be the chair of the King and Sox are fully committee activities, as the audit show.

Shady's partner in with King's company knows full tough, his firm will lose the account. by keeping proper distance, substance, don't ask/don't recommendations that

self-disclosure. If this sounds ethology of rats that makes catch.

contends that internal not a deterrent especially when choose to commit a company with fraud is unlikely to

accounting firms books prepared company typically negotiated by Sox. the auditors are the auspices of the the board, and meet the audit committee in the room. This fiction than fact. his closest confidant audit committee. aware of all audit Sox is controlling

charge of the engagement well, that if he gets too So he joins the rats' nest, observing form over tell, and making control the honest employees, but that keep King, Fats and Sox clean to the public eye.

Shady often relies on a Stinky LLP to get sanitized legal opinions on highly suspect financial structures and tax positions. As long as the form is proper, King and Fats buy their protection through legal, consulting and audit fees. If wrongdoing is discovered, Shady reaches a settlement agreement with the regulatory agency, pays a small fine, gets its wrist slapped, and then enjoys feeding on your cheese as the audit fees are distributed to the partners.

RAT PATROL

Follow reports in the financial press and on the Internet regarding corporate fraud that goes undetected by accounting firms – both the small, and, the marquee firms. None of the firms wants to be the next Arthur Anderson. Be particularly concerned when companies change auditors. Question the stated reasons for such change. Examine the trends in audit fees that are reported in SEC disclosures.

CHAPTER 16

Regulators/Lobbyists/Think Tanks—
"Recycle PhD"

In the city, given the absence of rat-eating wild mammals and
great numbers of birds of prey, the natural predator of the rat is
the exterminator.

Rats: Observations on the History and Habitat
of the City's Most Unwanted Inhabitants, 2004

he members of King's Inner and Outer Courts only
can be effective in stealing your cheese if they are not
exterminated in the process. Therefore, they must cycle
in and out of government to manage the regulatory functions,
and ensure a hefty payday when back in the private sector. Thus,
Recycle PhD is not an additional rat; rather, he is on temporary
leave from the King's Inner or Outer Court. He also may be a
former politico who now is enjoying the fruits of his legislative
favors by serving as a lobbyist for the King.

The revolving door from the positions that regulate business
and influence legislation to the companies that are regulated is a
perfect ingress and egress for rats. Whenever King's favorite party
(Democrat or Republican) is in office, the rats from his Court
move from their corporate positions to positions of regulatory
influence. When the party in power changes, the regulatory rats
move back to the corporations, the law firms, the lobbying firms
and the think tanks. Hence, Recycle is adept at moving on and off

the federal or state payrolls, and on and off the payrolls of King, Ratti, Serpente, Churn, and VC.

Recycle feeds off the cheese of taxpayers, as well as shareholders and consumers. Indeed, Recycle may help increase the stock price of King's company, so you may actually benefit from his actions if you own the stock. Recycle is reallocating wealth from those who do not feed him to those who do.

As a regulator, Recycle will work in the executive branch of government. He will oversee the departments that issue permits to King's company, regulate the investment community, oversee tax and fiscal policy development, procure goods and services for the government, oversee labor regulations, and initiate legislative bills with politicos in the legislative branch. When working as a regulator, the taxpayers will directly incur Recycle's pay and benefits, and indirectly pay again through pork to, and poor regulation of, King's company.

Recycles who play the lobbyist game are often JDs rather than PhDs. As a lobbyist, Recycle is paid directly by King's company. Recycle would not remain on the payroll for long if he did not deliver the goods. Recycle will foster legislation that aids the company. But this is an easy task because the politicos also are dependent on the same legislation being passed. King feeds Recycle as a lobbyist. King feeds the politicos with campaign contributions. Recycle and the politicos pay back King with contracts and favorable legislation.

Spend some time at the general aviation terminal at Reagan Airport in Washington D.C. or in the dining room of any upper-end eatery inside the beltway. Your stomach will turn, when you recognize that you are paying for the airplanes, the white tablecloth dinners, the fees of the lobbyists and the salaries of the regulators/legislators. In fact, you are paying the entire check by higher taxes and higher prices for goods and services.

As a think tank rat, Recycle's Doctor in Philosophy pays off handsomely. Not all Recycles have PhD's, but those who do are able to move back and forth to the Washington DC think tanks. This advanced degree enables Recycle to display his pedigree and provides an aura of legitimacy as he pontificates. Dr. Recycle's think tank will be funded by the King's company to produce scholarly reports that support the King's objectives for legislation. This is a convenient resting place for Recycle while he is waiting to return to the government payroll. As long as Recycle pumps out research that ends up with the right recommendations, the funding support continues from the King. This is transference at its best. Getting someone else with credentials to   support your cause is a powerful propaganda tool.

The so-called independent research activities of Recycle PhD become open bi-lateral gratuities, just like those given to vendors and contractors. We normally think of researchers and scientists as being above the behavior of rats. A major study, funded by the National Institutes of Health and released in Nature, studied the ethics of 3,000 researchers. The results, reported in the *Wall Street Journal* (Regalado 2005), found that 33% of scientists engaged in at least one of ten behaviors considered to be unethical. Interestingly

15.5% mentioned that they changed the design or the results of a study in response to pressure from a funding source. The lead author of the study stated that he wanted to understand how scientists' behavior was influenced by funding. Given that Recycle, a highly developed, intelligent rat, would never admit to unethical behavior, the statistic in this survey is undoubtedly understated.

Recycle, PhD is an important rat in the King's Outer Court. He steals your cheese in so many different ways: You are nibbled by higher taxes, lack of regulation (or misapplied regulation), poor legislation, higher product costs and inefficient government. But remember, the short-term stockholder of King's company will be a winner. This is why Recycle is so important to Churn, Hedgy, Mute and Privy. Recycle has the ability to move the stock in the short run, and that is how these rats make their money. Each hold the other rat's tail in its mouth forming a complete circle. And this closed circle has become formally known by ethologists as "the circle of the rat king."

RAT PATROL

Recycle can be easily identified by the Rat Patrol by examining his or her resume. Recycle will show a merry-go-round of activity of "public service" + lobbying + regulatory oversight + board membership + think tank membership + author offering advice. Googling Recycle would result in hundreds, if not thousands of information points, since this is what Recycle is best at--elevating his or her importance via PR exposure.

Hedge Funds Hire Lobbyists to Gather Tips in Washington

As federal authorities try to crack down on illegal trading using secrets leaked from companies, some hedge-fund managers are tapping another source of information: the corridors of the Capitol.

Hedge funds are finding that Washington can be a gold mine of market-moving information, easily gathered by the politically connected. The funds are hiring lobbyists – not to influence government, but to tell them what it's going to do. Several lobbying firms are ramping up their "political intelligence" units and charging hedge funds between $5,000 and $20,000 a month for tips and predictions.

Wall Street Journal Dec 8, 2006
Copyright © 2006 Dow Jones & Company Inc.

CHAPTER 17
Politico—"The Honorable Scurvy"

To avoid disputes, water voles will mark out their territory by leaving piles of feces at the water's edge. The latrines convey scent messages to other voles [to stay away].

Water Vole – *Arvicola terrestris*
***World of Animals,* 2003**

The interface between the politico and the CEO is shrouded by darkness. The activities are kept nocturnal so that you do not see the rats at the height of their feeding frenzy. But there is plenty of evidence that the rats are around, as you smell the feces that ring the territory of the politico. Open bi-lateral gratuities are the norm for King to receive favorable legislation and regulation. The Honorable Scurvy's primary goal is to be reelected at the federal, state or local level. To achieve this goal, Scurvy must build his war chest of campaign contributions, and pad his government income with free goods. Rather than a direct deposit from King Rat, appearances are better if the money is laundered through a "go-to" person, or from a member of the King's Outer Court. Check out the level of contributions to campaigns, inaugural events, and fund raising activities from Ratti, Serpente, Charlie, Churn, Hedgy, Mute, Privy, Hunter and Shady. All of these firms, skimming from the profits of the company, spend a portion of their windfall to keep the climate right in government circles to continue the feeding and to keep the exterminator away.

The Honorable Scurvy says that there is no favoritism given to those who contribute to his or her campaign, who provide honoraria, or who provide rides on private jets to exotic locations for fact-finding tours. Scurvy says there is no need to hire a lobbyist in order to achieve legislative changes. King says that any contributions made are for the purpose of electing representatives who will grow the economy and promote economic freedom.

Nothing can be farther from the truth. This is rat-chatter at its finest.

What is apparent is the merging of the political and the corporate realms. The corporate CEO is learning from the politician that mediocrity must be disguised, particularly when the potential remuneration is so large. By taking care of each other, working under the cover of darkness, and eating as much cheese as possible, they can retain their positions and enjoy the wealth. This is not conspiracy, but rather individuals operating in their own best interest.

The link between King and Scurvy works very well. The feces surrounding Scurvy are allowed to ferment nicely over time. The smell of these piles signals others to stay away. There is no way to challenge him for reelection because his war chest is full with cheese that was rightfully yours, but ended up in his domain. Scurvy may smell, but he is unbeatable!

Crime in the Suites

The fallacies of our era are on the table now, visible for all to see, but the follies are unlikely to be challenged promptly-- not without great political agitation. The other obvious deformity exposed by Enron is the insidious corruption of democracy by political money. The routine buying of politicians, federal regulators and laws does not constitute a go-to-jail scandal since it all appears to be legal. But we do have a strong new brief for enacting campaign finance reform that is real. The market ideology has produced the best government that money can buy. The looting is unlikely to end so long as democracy is for sale.

Nation February 4, 2002

Copyright © 2002 The Nation

RAT PATROL

A high percentage of career politicians fall into this category--so the Rat Patrol can assume that a politician is Scurvy, unless proven otherwise. The only politicians that are exempt are those who recommend (1) eliminating pork, (2) cutting the salary and benefits of legislators, and (3) establishing strict term limits.

Section III

Breed and Feed

The avarice of mankind is insatiable.

Aristotle, c. 336 B.C.

The total existence of a rat is to "breed and feed." These are the rat's only interests.

From John Stuart Mill's work in the 19th century, on what we now call economics, came the concept of economic man. Mill's economic man had four interests: accumulation, leisure, luxury and procreation (Persky 1995). Said another way, economic man's only interests were to "breed and feed."

For King Rats to "feed" they must have a breeding ground that facilitates the accumulation of your cheese. Therefore, we will examine first the breeding ground and then turn to the feast.

CHAPTER 18
The Breeding Ground

Ships are but boards, sailors but men, there be land-rats, and water-rats, water-thieves and land-thieves.

Shylock
The Merchant of Venice, Act I, Scene III
William Shakespeare
1564-1616

The breeding ground for the King and his Court is the large organization. It could be government, corporate, non-profit or union. The organization must have four characteristics to become a breeding ground:

- First, the organization must be of sufficient size to enable personal weakness to be hidden.
- Second, it must have sufficient wealth (assets and income potential) to make pillaging worthwhile.
- Third, its ownership must be distant and fragmented to limit oversight.
- Fourth, the risk of extermination of the King Rat must be low.

Size

The large organization is more vulnerable to infestation because layers of management enable feeding while the competent employees operate the company. The more bureaucracy the greater the potential for infestation. Rats feed, but they do not like to work. The actual work of the organization is left to those who make the organization viable. For this reason alone, nearly all government entities are severely infested. Large corporations, as well, tend to harbor rats at high levels.

The King and members of his Inner Court spend most of their time on personal matters, leaving others to be concerned with company business. With sufficient layers of management to distance themselves from the day-to-day activities, they have the freedom to work on feeding themselves. To survive, they need to operate behind a curtain of secrecy that is difficult to pull off in a small organization. If a member of the Inner Court finds himself in a position that has accountability and real responsibility, he will restructure to put another person in that position, so that others can be blamed for shortcomings. That is why you rarely see rats in direct operating, engineering and sales positions that have true accountability. These jobs are for the commoners, not for members of the Court. In *The Post Truth Era*, Keyes (2004) observed that the mobility and anonymity of contemporary life creates a breeding ground for dishonesty. The major corporation, with today's communication technology, provides for such conditions.

Wealth

Rats have a very sensitive sense of smell that leads them to a food source. The larger the potential feeding ground (wealth and power) the greater the potential for infestation. Having a target with significant assets and income is important. Just like the answer to the question to the bank robber: Why do you rob banks? -because that's where the money is, a King Rat will gravitate to where there is plenty of food. The King needs to tap into the asset base of the company, so that he can distribute the assets to his Court.

Companies with high revenues and complex cost structures are excellent breeding grounds. Profits are less important. Indeed, a King Rat will reduce profit by increasing costs, which end up in the pockets of himself and his Court.

The creation of value is irrelevant. King Rats operate one quarter at a time. Long-term strategy can be made up by Spin and Squealer to mesmerize Wimpy. Once the food source has been fully exploited, the rats abandon ship and move on to the next food source.

Distant/Fragmented Ownership

Rats run rampant in alleys feeding on garbage rather than within homes and restaurants. The alley represents a breeding ground with less direct ownership. While rats would not be tolerated in a home or restaurant, the alley is a common area, owned by the city and uninhabited by predators (humans) during the nightly feeding.

For the same reason, King Rats are more prevalent in the modern corporation with shareholdings spread across many individuals and institutions. No ethical owner wants a King Rat running his company. With contemporary corporate ownership, the shareholders are more distant and fragmented. These owners don't see the rats and they tend not to exercise their governance rights. The increased ownership and rapid trading of stock by hedge funds and mutual funds have exacerbated this trend. They operate more as renters than owners, and, as renters, they could care less about the long-term prospects for the company. They only care about getting the direction of stock price movement correct for as long as they hold the stock. Such ownership results in the control shifting from owners to managements.

As with the size characteristic, the "ownership" of government entities provides an even more fertile breeding ground. Here the owners are the voters who are extremely distant and fragmented. The vested interest among those in both elected and appointed positions is to take and redistribute your cheese to those in position to feed them, e.g. campaign contributors, grantors of favors, and future employers. This is the proven way to reelection or reappointment.

Low Risk of Extermination

The fourth characteristic of the breeding ground is that it provides cover for the rats and minimizes their chance of being caught stealing your cheese. Again, the modern corporation and regulatory environment provide cover for rats to thrive without serious risk of being caught. Similarly, government officials learn how to stretch the rules and how to seek protective cover when challenged. Rats are extremely wily and difficult to catch. They have calculated the cost/benefit--the risk of extermination versus the rewards of continued feeding. With the potential for wealth due to the explosion of CEO salaries and the payoff for government service, the cost/benefit increasingly favors rat-like behavior.

The steroid scandal in Major League Baseball is a clear

illustration of the inducements to such behavior. As long as the risk of getting caught was low, those who stood to gain were the juiced players who garnered large salary increases for hammering the ball. The losers were those who played by the rules, as they were at a competitive disadvantage. Only when the risk of extermination increased, did the fraudulent behavior subside.

Making it to the Big Show in baseball is now worth several million dollars annually. Playing in the minors, even at the level of Triple-A, is to live at a subsistence level. Therefore, the reward for cheating has increased, and the temptation for steroid use to stay competitive has increased.

A large organization such as the modern corporation or government bureaucracy is more exploitable by rats than Major League Baseball. To make it in the Majors, even with steroids, you still need talent. So, the number of rats eligible to enter the pool is highly restricted by this talent requirement. Therefore, baseball is not a good breeding ground for rats as long as the risk of extermination is maintained. The reason is that a rat cannot hide on the baseball diamond. He must have a high level of ability even without performance enhancing drugs. He must "walk the talk." However, the modern corporation is different because of the first characteristic of the breeding ground, the ability to hide, allows for a much broader pool of players. A CEO can make millions per year, just like the Major League player, but have no talent whatsoever. All that is needed is the willingness to exploit the weak and the trusting.

Periodically throughout history, infestation has become plague. Many would argue that we experienced a plague in the 2008 financial meltdown. Only when plague occurs does enforcement increase, resulting in the third and fourth conditions (limited oversight and low risk of extermination) being withdrawn temporarily. When some rats are exterminated or when ownership oversight tightens, the rats will move to another breeding ground (the conditions are once again relaxed). This is why we tend to see cycles in the degree of infestation within corporate America. An explosion of major fraud cases characterized the 1980's. Once again, in the early 2000's we saw a resurgence of fraud cases. In 2008, an explosion of fraudulent behavior has taken down the financial markets. Rat infestation was occurring all of the time in corporations and in government. Only when the infestation reaches plague proportions do we sit up and take notice. In response to plague, the Justice Department established a special task force in 2002 to crack down on corporate fraud. Over a three year period this task force charged over 900 individuals in more than 500 corporate fraud cases. (Solomon and Squeo 2005). After the "fire" is extinguished from the crisis of 2008, the corporate fraud crackdown will be resumed -- at a much larger scale.

However, these cases represent only the visible manifestations. Remember, rats operate below ground and only emerge under the cover of darkness. It is what you cannot see that should be of even greater concern. This book is not only about the Ken Lays, the Bernie Ebbers', the Dennis Kozlowskis, the John Rigas', the notorious Wall Street CEOs, et al -- as these cases have been discussed ad nausea. These individuals are simply visual manifestations of the King and his Court, and they represent those few who have fallen into traps.

Rather, the focus is on the less visible signs of infestation, where the rats are skimming and the damage is limited to avoid the spotlight. This is a far more costly infestation than the marquee crooks that make the *Wall Street Journal*. Rats congregate where there is little incentive for calling the exterminator, as they do not want to attract attention. Those in power want to keep the breeding ground active, since they are enjoying your cheese and don't want the supply disrupted. Too much infestation draws attention and dilutes the opportunity for feeding. Too much control would cut off their supply of cheese. For those in power, the level of infestation needs to be carefully maintained so that they can continue to enjoy feeding.

The ideal condition for a rat is to thrive under the cover of darkness, to steal sufficient cheese, but not to "bite too many babies" for fear of bringing in the exterminators. True rats know how far they can push the envelope. Those who push too far are eaten alive by other rats or are exterminated. We saw in 2008 an example of rats who have pushed too far by putting the US economy at risk. Many will be eaten by others (mergers and acquisitions), some will be exterminated (bankruptcy), and still others will survive to feed again--thanks to government bailout.

CHAPTER 19
The Feast

Thus, a scientist doing fieldwork in Africa came upon the carcase of an elephant, cause of death unknown. He diarized the sequence of events and found that in two weeks there was virtually no trace of the former mound of flesh and bones. First on the scene were the super-scavengers, the jackals, hyenas and vultures. They were followed by a variety of carrion-eaters of smaller sizes, including insects. Hyenas crunched the bones, except the skull, and rats gnawed what the hyenas left. The excrement from the scavengers and the detritus from their endless feeding fertilized the soil beneath and around the site of the carcase, and finally vegetation stimulated by the natural fertilizers grew up rank and tall, drawing a veil over any residue.

Just Like an Animal, 1978

he feast of a King Rat and his Court typically takes about five years to consume until the food source is depleted. However, this is an average, and the time frame in your company or organization would depend upon the degree of deviance of your King Rat. The timing of when your specific cheese is stolen is dependent on your stakeholder position and your level of threat to the King.

The King Rat and his Court are enjoying your cheese. This is where they may differ from the Urban Brown Rats whose favorite foods are fresh, frozen or canned meats, fish or pet foods and bacon. In fact, the favorite main course of the Brown Rat would be a fish-oil fried hamburger wrapped in bacon (Hendrickson 1983). Watch out for this on the menu of the executive dining room.

Let the meal begin!

Hors D'oeuvres—Cheese Dreams; Fried Mozzarella Sticks; Toasted Cheese Logs

For hors d'oeuvres, the King will feast on a selection of cheese-rich specialties that form his basic salary and bonus package. This selection of hors d'oeuvres far exceeds any reasonable compensation. The salary and bonus levels are set by the compensation committee of the board, lead by Fats. H. Hunter will recommend a very rich package, to acknowledge the superiority of the candidate selected to be King Rat. Subsequent package increases will be developed by the King himself with the assistance of Triple-R and outside human resource consultants.

Of course the board "demands" superior performance from its CEO and needs to justify its selection of CEO as being in the top quartile with a commensurate salary and bonus. This ratcheting up of salaries and bonuses has resulted in multimillion-dollar pay packages to very mediocre and even incompetent CEOs.

Raising the salaries and bonuses of the King and his Court raises the general and administrative expense on the company's income statement. To offset such increases, the King must compensate by holding down merit and cost of living increases for the workforce and eliminating jobs. This is accomplished with the help of Ratti. The effectiveness of the King as a cost-cutter is broadcasted widely to the investment community by Spin working with Wimpy.

You have no chance--your cheese hasn't been moved--it's been stolen. The King dreams about cheese, he fries you and sticks it to you, and then he rolls you like a toasted cheese log!

Soup—Quick Cheese Soup*

On top of salary and bonus, the King recommends to the board the long-term incentive compensation plan to enrich himself and his Court. These are cash awards, stock option grants, restricted stock grants and other forms of deferred compensation.

The King Rat especially likes cash compensation awards for himself and his favorite vassals. These special awards can be given when the company's performance is horrible, and the formulae for incentive compensation awards calculate to zero. In this way there is no need for the board to give the awards to all of the managers in the company eligible for incentive compensation. Rather, they can target the awards solely to the King and those of his choosing without running afoul of the securities regulations. The cash is out of the company and into the personal investment portfolios of the King and his Court.

Stock-based rewards are thought by many to be a function of how well the stock performs. Wrong again! If the stock market is lifting all boats because of strong GDP growth or higher prices in the industry sector of the King's company, then the King Rat and his Court strike gold regardless of their performance. They will cash out their options and stock grants for tens and even hundreds of millions of dollars. They may be the worst managers in their industry. But that's irrelevant.

Once the company's stock price is high, the board will give restricted stock because they know that options would be worthless given the prospects for the company. In this way, the King and his Court cash out regardless of future movements of

---

*Garnished with chopped parsley (but declined by most rats).

the stock. If the stock price declines (for whatever reason), the board will throw in more options or re-price old options to give management "more incentive."

In exchange for providing this fabulous wealth to the King, the board is given increased fees for service and other perks. King makes sure that there is quid pro quo. Also, as CEOs themselves, the board members have raised the bar for stock compensation packages in their own companies.

King and Fats try to move the stock with their forecasts, Potemkin press releases, and other propaganda so that they can cash out of their options at an opportune time before the normal investors realize that the company is in the tank. Even though the periods when they can exercise their options are restricted, this is not a problem, as they control the information flow. Their goal is to skim off for themselves that which should go to the shareholders in higher dividends or a higher stock price. Stock based incentive plans are the "quick" way to fabulous wealth!

Salad—Cheese Ring Salad**

King and Fats now have their basic pay package and stock based compensation, but they must secure their positions by cementing relationships with FOKers and FOCers.

King and Fats employ consultants when internal employees could do the job. Vendors and contractors are given favored positions, human resource consultants justify pay increases, and executive search firms are brought in whenever promotion opportunities arise.

This skimming of the company treasury propels King and

**Refrigerate until ready to serve.

Fats onto other boards and establishes superb references for other lucrative positions. Remember that King and Fats don't gain anything by giving you a raise, or treating you fairly. In fact, treating you like a human being hurts King and Fats. If they give you anything, there is less for them to give to the FOKers and the FOCers. As well, they would not get credit for reducing head count and overhead costs (even though consultant costs increase and the company loses its internal capabilities). This siphoning of corporate funds is undetectable as it is rolled into the cost of goods sold using creative accounting by Sox and attested to by Green I. Shade.

Who loses? The shareholders, the honest vendors, and the employees. King Rat will ice you--just like his salad!

Main Course***--Veal Cordon Bleu, Potatoes Au Gratin, Puffed Cheese Balls

Finally, the main course. King and Fats not only feast on their salary, cash bonuses, stock-based compensation, and future prospects based on payments to FOKers and FOCers--they also need to make more money on their investments. This is where Churn, Hedgy, Mute, Privy and Wimpy come into the picture.

After all, King and Fats did not give lucrative investment banking business to Churn & Burn without expecting anything in return. Nor did they give Hedgy, Mute and Privy inside information for them to reap millions in fees, without gratuities in return. Neither would be rational behavior.

***Macaroni and Cheese or Grilled Cheese Sandwich may be substituted as the main course for junior rats such as Squealer and Wimpy.

The bi-lateral gratuities come in many forms, are difficult to trace, and impossible to prosecute. These might take the form of favored positions in initial public offerings, better mortgage rates on their personal homes, a golden parachute if King agrees to merge or sell his company, and inside information on other transactions unrelated to the King's company.

Wimpy issues glowing investment reports on King's company, especially highlighting the superior management. This raises the stock price of King's company and enriches his options. Churn gives King and Fats inside deals on personal investments. Hedgy, Mute and Privy provide King and Fats with inside information on market moves. King and Fats give board seats to the brother-in-law of Hedgy, and contribute to Mute's and Privy's favorite charities so that Mute can become an honorary board member or Privy's three-year-old can get into a prestigious mid-town Manhattan nursery school. The combinations and permutations are endless.

All of the members of the King's Court use their privileged positions to increase wealth and power at your expense. The wealth transfer from these bi-laterals dwarfs those from the preliminary courses. This is truly the main course!

Dessert—New York Cheese Cake

What would be a feast without the dessert table?

The dessert for the King Rat is the payoff when he is asked to leave the company (which is inevitable). He would have been granted an employment contract by the board when he joined. This contract typically gives King a lump-sum payout based on three to five years of salary and bonuses, lucrative pension benefits, healthcare for life, and, frequently, use of corporate aircraft and a company apartment.

The King Rat wins whether he stays or leaves. If he is forced out, he will be given the value of his contract (which frequently has a rolling term feature that always provides for the maximum payout). On top of this contractual amount, the board will offer a discretionary "golden handshake", so he goes quietly with the company's propaganda machine intact, the secrets secure, and the board's reputation enhanced for acting decisively. This "handshake" is really to protect the board members from revealing their incompetence.

If you think that these packages are limited to celebrity CEOs, you are wrong again! Mediocre chiefs are given exit packages in the tens of millions of dollars. Perhaps their boards' compensation committees are basing the payouts on the size of cheese cake served at an 8th Avenue, mid-town deli.

Professor Yermack (2005b) studied the golden handshakes given to 179 CEOs departing Fortune 500 companies between 1996 and 2002. He found that the average package was $5.4 million, with 19 exceeding $10 million. CEOs that were fired were given a golden handshake 83% of the time. Fired CEOs received larger packages than those leaving voluntarily. Remember--this is totally discretionary!

And you thought that you could not have your cake and eat it too!

After-Dinner Drinks and Cuban Cigars

I'll bet that before you turned the page you thought the feast was over. If so, you are not thinking like a rat. Always remember, the gluttony of a rat is never satisfied.

The King Rat will drink to his wealth and power, offer a toast to the members of his Court and pass around the Cuban cigars that he smuggled into the country on his G-IV. The one reward that the King still lacks is his legacy. He must cement his legacy for all to honor for his remaining days as a live rat and for his eulogy upon his untimely death. Death is always untimely for a worshipped business leader.

Whether you are an employee, a retiree, a customer, a legitimate vendor or a shareholder, King Rat has stolen your cheese. But you are never to know, because then you would not forever hold him in high esteem. You see, he not only wants your cheese, but he also wants your adoration.

How might this be achieved, you ask, given the reputation of a rat? The cunning of a rat is that you will never know that he was a rat. King Rat employs a ghost writer (Spin is very good at this job) to prepare his memoirs and other books glorifying his management ability. King receives a princely sum as an advance from the publishing company. King's inflated ego needs stroking by the celebrity-starved public, always questing for hero-worship. So King will have his agent book him on the television and radio talk show circuit to promote the book, but even better to build his legacy.

These books litter the shelves of business libraries. They rehash old themes and update them with the management jargon of the day. Typically they are written by aging King Rats, Rattis, Churns and Scurvys. The subjects are always the same: leadership principles, management change and how to gain wealth. The answers are always the same: the King was a great leader (and he knows how to turn you into a great leader); change is good (borrowed from the politicos); it is your failure to change that is causing you to fail (your cheese has moved, and it was all your fault); and that you can gain great wealth if you follow his lead. This is complete puffery, because he would never admit what made him wealthy, because it would lead to incarceration.

These books are big sellers because they are read and lauded by all of the other Kings, Fats, Triple-Rs, Soxs, Snakes, Spins, Squealers, Rattis, Serpentes, Charlies, Churns, Wimpys, Hedgys, Mutes, Privys, Hunters, Shadys, Recycles and Scurvys. With so many wealthy and powerful individuals as witness to the wisdom of the latest book, King's place in history is cemented.

As they lie in their burrows in the sands of Palm Beach and Nantucket, they are satisfied. They have received their earthly rewards--fabulous wealth, power, celebrity and an enduring legacy. They offer a toast to themselves and continue to blow smoke at you!

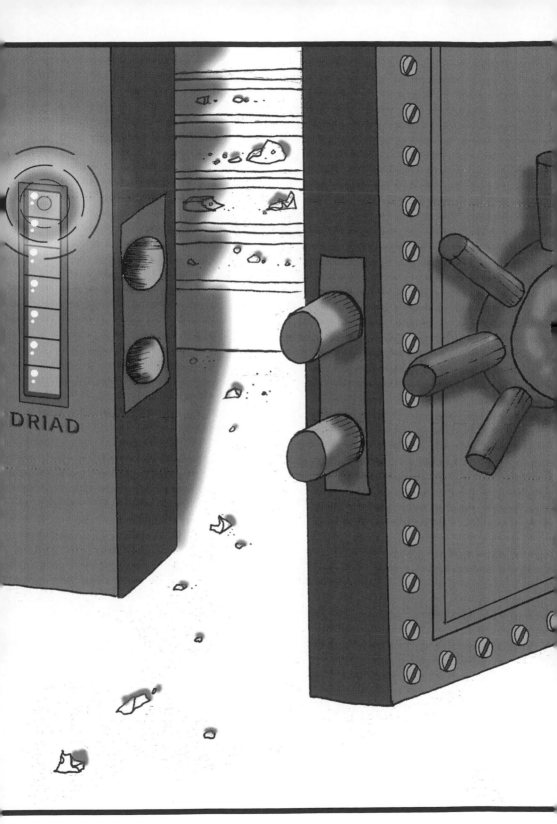

Section IV

It's A Matter of Degree

The philosophers, I am sure, have somewhat the impression that the economists are avoiding what they regard as the basic issue, namely, the value judgments that affect and enter into private and public policy. And by value judgments, the philosophers do not mean relative exchange value. They mean "moral" or "ethical" values. The philosophers in my opinion are correct.

Milton Friedman
1912-2006

When you consider the ethical standards that pervade your organization and are promoted by your leadership, two fundamental questions arise. First, how infested is your organization? Second, what is the degree of deviance of your leaders? Only then will you be able to determine the **DRIAD**.

CHAPTER 20
Degree of Infestation

Just as a dog can support a large but limited number of fleas, ticks and tapeworms, so can the legal and business systems support parasitic individuals, lawyers and businesspeople, those who individually violate the fundamental norms of fairness--up to a point and with increasing difficulty and dysfunction as the system approaches that point.

Journal of Corporation Law, 2004

J ust how infested is your organization? There are common signposts that indicate how far along your organization is toward destruction. Fortunately, the degrees of cultural pathology have been studied by academics providing the warning signs. Many of these signs will strike a nerve as you lie in bed, staring at the ceiling and wondering why your organization is self-destructing.

3rd Degree Infestation

When you see the signs of the presence of rats, such as rat droppings in the sink, gnarled toilet paper in the bathroom, and dishevelment in the kitchen--you can expect that you have a problem. If there is one rat, there are usually more. If you call pest control soon enough, you may be able to exterminate the creatures before the damage is too severe. The household can be restored to normalcy without much cost.

This is 3rd degree infestation, when the rats have not harmed the people or the infrastructure and any minor damage can be easily fixed. No one has been bitten yet, but the signs of trouble are evident.

This is the initial stage when a King Rat enters the organization at a high level and begins to plan his infestation. If the board removes this individual at an early stage, the damage can be limited. This requires that the board has not been tainted, and its members are sufficiently savvy to identify the signs of rats. In a previously rat-free company, a King Rat new to the organization will take at least two years of sniffing around before exhibiting outward signs of rat-like behavior. You need to be quite perceptive to smell a rat at this early stage.

Third-degree infestation also could occur at lower levels within an organization, such as at the department level. Rats entering at lower levels (that do not have a King's Court to join) are isolated and are left to inflict damage on their own departments. As long as the rats are not promoted, such individuals can last for many years making your life uncomfortable, but their damage to the total corporation will be limited.

2nd Degree Infestation

If the chairman of the board and the CEO are both rats (or if they are the same individual), then the degree of infestation is allowed to progress rapidly as internal control mechanisms are rendered ineffective. This is second-degree infestation, and a sign of deep trouble for the organization. The King Rat begins to develop his Court. The King identifies the individuals who are willing to sell their souls for promises of big rewards. In the 2nd degree there are outward signs of fraudulent behavior by the King and his Court. These include the purging of independent employees who are branded as troublemakers, declining financial performance, and the reduction or elimination of benefits to employees and retirees. Although insiders can see this deterioration, the King's propaganda machine provides a smoke screen to avoid detection from outside. Any insider brave enough to confront the King or his mercenaries will be eliminated savagely.

The infestation will continue to expand as the number of rats grows and drives out the honest, hard working employees from the organization. The process may take several years to accomplish, but as long as there is sufficient cheese, the King Rat will continue feeding.

1st Degree Infestation

Infestation in the first degree is normally fatal to the company. This is the plague. The King and his Court are fully in place and they are executing outright theft of corporate assets and continued elimination of competent personnel. Plagues cause severe damage and destruction, kill off the non-rats, and lead to eventual failure of the organization. The organization infested to the 1st degree is pathologically politicized. The tension in the air is so thick that you can feel it whenever the rats come near you. Your blood pressure rises and your hair curls. This is a truly sickening environment for any spiritually healthy individual.

In *The Secret Handshake*, Professor Kathleen Reardon (2001, 20-21) listed five tell-tale signs of an organization that is pathological:

- Flattering of those in power coupled with abusiveness toward people in lower positions.
- Information messaging--communication by "hinting."
- Verbal backstabbing.
- No one is valued--everyone is dispensable.
- "Fake left, go right" strategy--leading others in the wrong direction to make oneself look good.

In *The Paranoid Corporation*, Cohen and Cohen (1993) found that a close look at such a corporation will uncover suspicion, lack of trust, significant fear of outsiders, and security as a primary concern.

In *Good to Great*, Jim Collins (2001) spent most of his time discussing great companies; however, he does devote some words to companies that he says are in the "doom loop." These companies:

- Implement big programs, radical change efforts, dramatic revolutions, and chronic restructurings.
- Embrace fads.
- Demonstrate chronic inconsistency, lurching back and forth.
- Jump right into action without disciplined thought.
- Sell the future to compensate for the lack of results.

If these symptoms are prevalent in your organization, the rats are on the loose and you are infested to the 1st degree. Ethical employees feel great stress working in this highly politicized environment.

Your stress level builds because there is no outlet to blow off steam. The King's Court provides an impenetrable shield. Professor Reardon (2001) observed that in such organizations many topics become taboo, few people talk to the CEO or his direct reports, and formally sanctioned rules are only followed when convenient, rather than applied consistently.

Reardon classifies CEOs into types of individuals who are likely to be at the head of pathological organizations. In particular, she identifies a type of CEO, whom she calls "The Manueverer" as the best fit for a pathological political environment. The Manueverer is defined as a subtle operator rather than a street fighter. He looks for ulterior motives in others, has little regard for sanctioned rules, and relies on subliminal politics. If people get in the way, it is at their own peril.

If you see the warning signs posted by Reardon, Cohen and Cohen, and Collins, you have evidence of 1st degree infestation.

CHAPTER 21
Degree of Deviance

You only find out who is swimming naked when the tide goes out.

Warren Buffett

ot all chief executive officers exhibit the ethology of rats. For those who do, their degree of deviance can range from mild to extreme. This chapter will enable you to pinpoint the degree of deviance of the leaders of your organization. Once a rat, always a rat is a common expression. A CEO with low competence and little credibility is likely to continue and escalate his behavior because he has little to lose. Also, being a rat is a slippery slope. Once your cheese is tasted, the path to gluttony is all downhill.

There is an inverse correlation between competence of an organizational leader and his degree of deviance. The less competent a person is for the job, the higher degree of deviance. This is expected, since acting like a rat is the only way an incompetent person can get the job and maintain the job. The more competent leaders may use a mild degree of rat-like behavior to strengthen their positions, and increase their compensation. They may have been truly qualified for the position; however, they may further increase their rewards by acting like a King Rat.

Con Artists

There are plenty of con artists operating at all levels in our society, not just snake oil salesmen or rug merchants. The business of a con artist is to steal money from other people. We would all call con artists ratty, particularly those that prey on the weak and vulnerable. In *Fraud! How to Protect Yourself From Schemes, Scams and Swindlers* Bertrand (2000) described the traits of con men:

• Narcissistic, self-centered and grandiose.
• Large egos.
• Think they are too smart to get caught.
• Lack conscience or remorse.
• Insincere, shallow and superficial.

It is interesting to compare these characteristics to the deviant CEO and to many of our political leaders. Indeed, the King Rat is a con artist dressed in a suit.

Organized Crime Leaders

In organized crime families, the Don establishes his turf and extracts most economic rent for his own benefit. Keys to his success are the elimination of competition and the weeding out of those who refuse to pay up. The end result, in effect, is a licensing agreement between the Don and the shopkeeper that is enforced through power. The Don receives the benefit of all transactions, while the participants are able to survive by favor of the Don.

The Don addresses governmental oversight through payoffs to the police, judges and local politicians who serve at his pleasure. He maintains a storefront business as a means to express legitimacy. The Don operates with intermediaries so that when his underlings are caught, the link to the top cannot be established. Both organized crime families and gangs protect their turf by intimidation and violence, threatening any intruders.

The King Rat is a Don. He is an organized crime leader in a double-breasted suit.

Dictatorships

Saddam Hussein studied the ways of the rat to maintain power and control over the Iraqi people. Saddam neutralized opponents with the gassing of innocents, brutal slayings, and a loyal inner circle maintained by doling out gratuities. He became fabulously wealthy by fraudulent transactions such as the Oil-for-Food program. The "food" that was exchanged for the oil ended up in the palaces of the King Rat. His propaganda machine enabled him to control knowledge and communications.

Saddam was found in a rat hole. The routes followed by insurgents from Syria into central Iraq are called ratlines. Saddam sat in a cage during his trial.

These were the characteristics of Saddam Hussein:

• Vigilant preparedness to counter all attacks and personal threats.

• Hypersensitivity.

- Coldness and lack of emotional expression.
- Deep suspicion and distrust.
- Over-involvement in rules and details to secure control.
- Vindictiveness.
- Craving for information.

Actually, these were not written about Saddam Hussein. They were written about the traits of certain CEOs in *Unstable at the Top: Inside the Troubled Organization* (Kets de Vries and Miller 1987).

Picture the King Rat standing on the balcony, extolling the crowd, firing a rifle in the air, and dressed in a business suit.

. . . .

The con artist, the Don, the dictator, and the King Rat are in the same suit with the same mindset. They all use territory that they control as their personal kingdom to satisfy their own greed. Consider the personality traits of the leaders with whom you are most familiar. Then determine where they fit on the continuum of deviant behavior.

Find out who is in the suit in the corner suite. You may find him - once disrobed - swimming naked!

CHAPTER 22

The Degree of Rat Infestation and Deviance (DRIAD)

> *You don't need a weatherman to know which way the wind blows.*
>
> **Bob Dylan**
> **Subterranean Homesick Blues, 1965**

ith knowledge of the King and his Court and their methods, you are prepared to test the organizations with which you are most familiar. This test will establish the degree of rat infestation and deviance of the chief in your company, non-profit or other institution.

The **DRIAD** should be a required measure in external reporting, as an indication of the true state of affairs in an organization. Other measures are based on propaganda from the King and his Court--even those under the auspices of the SEC and the stock exchanges. The **DRIAD** would be informative to regulators, employees (former, existing and prospective), investors, regulators and law enforcement agencies. Obviously, the difficulty is to obtain a measure that is not contaminated by the rats themselves or their propaganda. Despite this challenge, the imperative is to quantify the **DRIADs** in organizations known to you. Unlike other measures with their disclaimers, the **DRIAD** would be a guarantee of future performance.

Once you are ready to test your organization, turn to the Appendix for instructions and test questions. You and your colleagues should test and calculate your scores independently, so that you can establish the mean and standard deviation of the **DRIADs** for your organization.

The mean of your scores (the average **DRIAD**) will tell you the degree of infestation of rats in your organization and the degree of deviance of your leaders. A helpful scale is presented on the following page to put your results in perspective.

The standard deviation of your scores is a function of two factors. The first is the effectiveness of the company's propaganda machine, preventing even insiders from knowing the extent of infestation and lack of leadership. This factor will understate the mean and also will cause great scatter of the results, as only those in the know will have a clear understanding of the severity of the problems. The second factor is how well the organization was run under prior management and how long the King Rat has been CEO. Organizations that were well run before the King assumed power would show a tight distribution of **DRIADs** in the early years of infestation. Everyone will recognize the difference in behavior between the CEOs. Conversely, if the previous management was weak, then your colleagues may not notice the continuing weakness. They will begin to believe that this is the norm. History will have been erased, and the ability to make comparisons diminished.

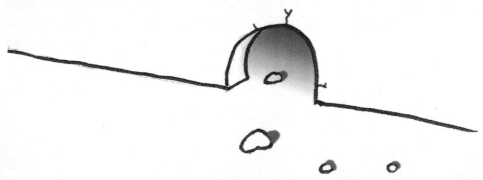

The **DRIAD** test consists of a total of 50 questions. The minimum "R" ("Rat") score is 0 and the maximum is 500. The following ranges of R scores indicate the degree of infestation and deviance in your organization:

Score	DRIAD	Description
0<R<50	1.0	Congratulations – Your organization is rat-free.
50<R<150	2.0	3rd Degree Infestation - Droppings are apparent.
150<R<200	3.0	Your cheese is being stolen.
200<R<300	4.0	2nd Degree Infestation - The rats are attacking daily.
300<R<350	5.0	Your organization is in dire straits.
350<R<450	6.0	1st Degree Infestation - Your organization is completely infested and your leadership pathological.
R>450	7.0	Bankruptcy is near – the rats soon will be abandoning ship.

Which way is the wind blowing in your organization? I am sure that you don't need a weatherman to help you calculate its **DRIAD**!

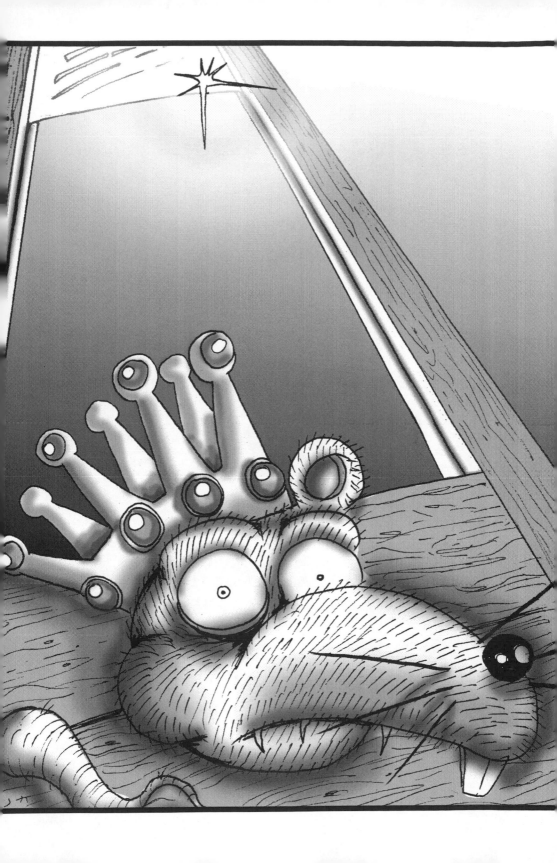

Section V

The Rat Killing

Manually operated guillotines for rodents are commercially manufactured and widely available.

Animals and the Law: A Source Book, 2001

hy is it so difficult to rid society of King Rats? The answer is that both the King Rats and their exterminators have dilemmas. Before we can clean house, we must address these dilemmas.

CHAPTER 23
The King Rat's Dilemma

Once you give up your ethics, the rest is a piece of cake.

J.R. Ewing, Dallas

nderstanding the King Rat's behavior does not require conspiracy theories. His dilemma is that he must act like a rat, or he would be unable to maintain his position of power and wealth.

The philosopher William James argued that humans have the power to will their own culturally defined boundaries. He believed that ethical standards and truth are relative concepts. If James were alive today, he likely would say that ethical behavior in business is defined by the corporate community and by investors (Bruno 2005). Unfortunately, what is considered acceptable ethical behavior in the corporate world has sunk to rat-like standards, because that is what is necessary to reach the pinnacle.

This is what some call ledger book morality (Keyes 2004). Although honesty is considered by some as all or nothing, many individuals pick and choose where and when to be honest. In today's society, compartmentalism is in vogue by our leaders, and most who practice compartmentalism believe it to be a virtue. They are able to separate the various rooms of their lives from one another--their business lives from their family lives, their behavior in public from their behavior in private, cheating on their income taxes, cheating on their spouses. As the ethical standards decline, rat-like behavior becomes justified, and even necessary, to survive.

The King Rat's dilemma is in fact a derivation of the Prisoners' Dilemma, a game theory attributed to Princeton mathematician A. W. Tucker. It describes why individuals make decisions that benefit themselves rather than the collective whole--and why selfishness is the rational decision.

In the Prisoners' Dilemma, two suspects are being interrogated about a crime in separate rooms. If one confesses and the other does not, the one who confesses will get a one-year sentence, and the other will get 10 years. If both confess, they will get five years each. If neither confesses, there will be no case, but they can be convicted of a lesser charge of two years.

The best collective outcome is if neither confesses, but since the other suspect may confess, the safest decision is for both of them to confess. The dilemma arises because the rational, self-interested individual should choose to confess, which is clearly contrary to the common good (Grant 2004).

Of course, the Prisoners' Dilemma is a one-time decision. However, a CEO must make continuous decisions, so clearly he should consider the common good. In fact, Adam Smith had a name for this: the discipline of continuous dealings (Tullock 1985). Adam Smith contended that continuous dealings would take care of cheating and encourage individuals to make decisions for the common good--to behave cooperatively. However, with today's corporate ownership and the revolving door of CEOs, Adam Smith's condition of continuous dealings is no longer operative.

Almost all interactions between human beings can be framed as Prisoners' Dilemmas because it is possible for one party, or all parties, to make a one-time gain by cheating. Tullock observed that in a competitive market, in which a person intends to remain, almost no one takes this opportunity because the cost of getting a reputation for cheating is too high (ibid.). However, if an individual has lost his reputation, there is little or no reason why he should cooperate with others in the future. Tullock further states, "Under these circumstances he should con people into games, and when he gets them in, the decision to play non-cooperatively may well be perfectly rational"

(ibid.,1079).

Therefore, a person who cheats will continue showing this behavior. The habitual criminal or shady businessman who continues to be shady is exhibiting rational behavior. Once they have a bad reputation, the cost of building up a reputation of reliability is extremely high (ibid.).

If there is only one person with whom you can play the game, both he and you will likely decide not to cooperate. As the number of people playing increases, the prospect of finding another partner exerts pressure to play cooperatively. Therefore, perfect competition is the way to ensure cooperation and mutually advantageous decisions. Adam Smith would agree with this. Unfortunately, we do not have this condition in place in the corner office or in the boardroom.

Only when long-term financial performance is the goal of a company, will an organization thrive with individuals of high ethical standards. Unfortunately, long-term performance is not the goal of today's owners--the mutual funds, the hedge funds and the private equity firms. The goal of these modern owners is, by moving the stock price up or down in the short-run, to extract cash from the business for themselves and their investors.

Therefore, the Prisoners' Dilemma rationally explains the self-interest of an individual to play against the larger collectivity. It is tempting for the individual to cheat, because the cost of cheating to the group as a whole is small, whereas the benefit of cheating to the individual is potentially large. However, the benefits remain large for only as long as the numbers of those cheating do not overwhelm the hosts. The irony is that cheaters depend upon the vast majority of people being honest for their cheating behavior to be successful. The basic concept of a working society assumes that a social contract is in place whereby individuals make a deal with society at large to behave cooperatively (Barash 2004). The King Rat takes advantage of this social contract for his own benefit.

In many business schools, the MBA students are required to take a course in ethics. The course is intended to act as a counterweight to neoclassical economics that teach the principles of self-interest in optimizing decisions: "In financial economic theory, rational agents are assumed to be material opportunists who will readily jettison honesty and integrity in favor of guile and deceit whenever the latter are more likely to maximize some payoff function; indeed, to act other than opportunistically is by this definition irrational" (Dobson 2003, 30). MBA students are quick to grasp this dilemma as they enter the corporate world.

When cheating and unethical behavior become the norm (whether it be steroids in baseball, or insider trading among chiefs), ethical individuals and ethical companies will not be able to compete. Any dishonest person can be a free-rider on the fairness of others, and such behavior can be very profitable (Atkinson 2004). Those individuals with ethics that operate in a market that encourages unethical behavior have only three choices (Hanson 1991):

• Bend the rules.

• Act ethically and accept the consequences.

• Work to change the incentives for unethical behavior.

The King Rat's real dilemma is when you choose the third option.

CHAPTER 24

The Exterminator's Dilemma

Rats!
They fought the dogs and killed the cats,
And bit the babies in the cradles,
And ate the cheeses out of the vats.
And licked the soup from the cook's own ladles,
Split open the kegs of salted sprats,
Made nests inside men's Sunday hats,
And even spoiled the women's chats,
By drowning their speaking
With shrieking and squeaking
In fifty different sharps and flats.

Robert Browning 1812-1889
The Pied Piper of Hamelin
Verse 2

hy the silence? What has happened to pest control? Why are the rats allowed to proliferate in today's society? Who has the freedom to speak out against the rats? Where are the exterminators? What is their dilemma?

The simple answer is that the King and his Court are individuals with incredible wealth, and individuals with wealth are highly sought after in today's society. Those with wealth, regardless if it was obtained honestly or by fraud, are the preferred members of boards of directors, trustees of non-profit institutions, and targets for political campaign contributions.

In *The Dark Side of Organizations and a Method to Reveal It* (Bella, King and Kailin 2003), the authors attempted to answer the question of how the chain of fraudulent behavior can be broken given the enormous transfer of wealth that perpetuates the behavior. They say that this can only be achieved through credible disruptions--independent inquires, questions, objections and challenges. But who will rise to create these credible disruptions?

John Kenneth Galbraith (2004) believed that government must step in to prevent the socially undesirable behavior of today's CEOs. Galbraith spoke of the remarkable trend toward self reward of CEOs. He argued that the public authority (the regulators) must deal with the problem of the abuse of management authority which enables personal enrichment at the expense of others. But aren't the regulators part of the problem?

The Dalai Lama (1999) suggested that ethical behavior is a universal responsibility, and that such universality leads to a commitment to the principles of honesty and justice. "Ethical discipline is indispensable because it is the means by which we mediate between competing claims of my right to happiness and others' equal rights" (ibid.,146). Ethical discipline "entails the cultivation of virtue" (ibid.). But who will cultivate this virtue?

Who, today, has the unfettered freedom to work our elected the this problem? Certainly officials and regulators are first line of defense; however, many of them are rats themselves. The others are the tenured faculty in universities, the charitable trusts, the foundations, the independent think tanks, the religious institutions, and the unions.

We depend upon these individuals and institutions to defend the public trust. These positions have the pulpits, and most often the vision, to see through the context that King Rats try to impose on us.

However, all of these organizations have boards of trustees with a fiduciary responsibility of ensuring that the organization continues. Whether it is called alumni development, charitable donations, foundation development or the collection basket, the most important job of the board and the executive director is fundraising. Naturally, the leadership of the organization does not want to bite the hand that feeds it. The president of a university, the chief executive of a charity, the pastor of a congregation, the executive director of a Washington DC think tank, and the Congressman all have the same dilemma. They will not keep their positions if funding declines.

Why the silence of those empowered to speak out against the personal enrichment of our corporate and civic leaders?

- Elected government officials won't criticize because soft money contributions and kickbacks from lobbyists depend on corporate funding.

- Government regulators won't criticize because they are appointed by elected officials and know what is expected of them. Besides, they want to recycle into lobbying or corporate positions.

- Universities won't criticize because corporations provide research grants and hire the product of the universities, the graduating student. Wealthy alumni CEOs sit on the board of trustees and fund the university's endowment. Only the most secure, tenured faculty may be immune from administrative pressures.

- Think tanks won't criticize because many depend on corporations for funding support.
- Charities won't criticize because their funding comes from corporations and wealthy executives who serve as board members and as major contributors.
- Union leaders won't criticize because they have their backdoor deals with the corporate King Rat, at the expense of the rank and file.

The sad aspect of the exterminator's dilemma is that the King Rats will proliferate until they start to kill the host. At the bottom of the cycle, when the plague is in full force, only then will the critics emerge because they realize that their feeding opportunities will end if the host dies. This is a tremendous cost to society. Infestation is very difficult to counter--especially when dealing with rats. This is indeed why we see the finger-pointing between government and the private sector when assessing blame for the 2008 financial crisis. The plague is in full force, and the rats are killing the host.

CHAPTER 25

Cleaning House

Faith in the ability of a leader is of slight service unless it be united with faith in his justice.

General George Washington Goethals
Chief Engineer of the Panama Canal
1858 -1928

here is hope for cleaning house...and that hope is you! The number of honest and ethical people far outnumber the rats. Those who want you to believe your cheese has been moved--when it really has been stolen--have temporarily drugged you. Rats depend upon the host (you) to continue to feed them, so that they can live in a parasitic relationship. They really don't want to kill you; they just want some of your cheese. The rats have been sufficiently cunning (until now) to keep the outrage of the host controlled.

In order to begin cleaning house, we must:

- Identify the problem of unethical behavior among political and corporate leaders, and reduce the incentives for such behavior.

- Maintain a high level of personal ethics (do not succumb to the rats), because there is hope for controlling the infestation.

- Insist that government officials do the job for which they were elected: to pass laws and to oversee the regulatory environment for the benefit of their constituents rather than the big donors.

- Insist upon term limits and the elimination of pensions for elected officials, so that representative government will consist of individuals who want to serve the people rather than themselves.

- Provide resources and tools for prosecutors to uncover fraud and convict the perpetrators.
- Exercise rights to elect directors of corporations who will serve the shareholder and not the management.
- Install union leaders who support the rank and file, rather than lining their own pockets.
- Encourage university professors, think tanks, and private foundations to find the truth rather than the answers that support their research grants.
- Promote religious leaders who not only preach honesty, integrity and humility to their congregations, but also practice these virtues in their own lives.
- Introduce ethics into the curricula for all students during their formative years.

Rodentologists have found that traps and poison only temporarily reduce rat populations (Hendrickson 1983). They discovered that competition was the best way to limit the number of rats: "Man should change the environment through better sanitation as to cause an increase in competition and predation; thereby,

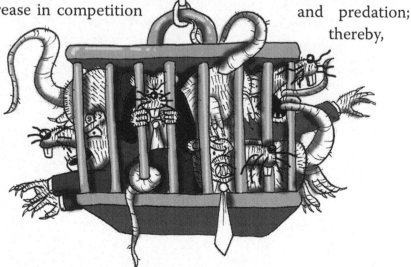

lowering the capacity of the environment to support rats" (ibid.,133). If you deny rats food, water and living space, they will compete violently and cannibalize one another.

Indeed the ultimate solution is for free markets and open competition to be allowed to function. Full disclosure, transparency, responsibility and accountability are necessary to shed light on our leaders. Taking ownership of the elective process and driving out the King Rats from political office is the necessary first step. Only then will the ownership process filter down to enable the corporate world to clean house.

OSTSCRIPT

The reader of this book might wonder: who do I believe best exemplifies the antithesis of the King Rat? What type of business leader does our economy need for sustainability? And, what virtues should we look for in leaders who seek high positions in government and business?

I choose to avoid naming a contemporary leader as the shining example, simply because the jury is still out on his or her ultimate performance. Some 40 years ago, I came upon an outstanding role model for leadership excellence when I was a graduate student in civil engineering and an officer in the U.S. Army Corps of Engineers. This leader was an American hero in the early 20th Century (and, even today, New Yorkers know his name, albeit from rush-hour traffic reports on metropolitan area bridges). He was a decisive leader, a brilliant engineer, an outstanding executive, a dedicated public servant and a person of true humility. His name is General George Washington Goethals, the builder of the Panama Canal and the first Civil Governor of the Panama Canal Zone.

A native of Brooklyn, New York, the son of Dutch immigrants, and an 1880 graduate of West Point, Goethals was appointed by President Theodore Roosevelt in 1907 to the Isthmian Canal Commission, and soon became the chairman and chief engineer of the Commission. He succeeded where his predecessors had failed. He overcame engineering challenges, organizational complexity, tropical diseases, and labor relations problems to complete the Canal nearly a year ahead of schedule.

Over the seven years of canal construction, he earned a reputation as a tough-minded, capable executive. Known to be an extremely hard worker who understood the details of his business, he demanded the highest standards of himself and those who worked under his command. He always required full authority for decision-making from his superiors, and he took full responsibility for the results.

What was different about Goethals, setting him apart from many great business leaders of the late 19th and early 20th centuries, was his reputation for high moral character and his uniform application of justice. "He was chief engineer, Governor, Judge and court of last recourse in the years he ruled the Isthmus" (New York Times 1928). He treated all who worked under his command with equal respect. Every Sunday, Goethals had an open-door session that was available to anyone who felt wronged. He treated all levels in the work force the same -- regardless of rank, economic status, nationality or color. After hearing complaints, he acted decisively. "As a man of great force and personality, he inspired complete confidence in the entire organization, and brought it together in harmony. The canal job came to be known as a model of efficient labor and industrial harmony, as well as sound engineering"(ibid.).

Lesser known, was how Goethals conducted himself around politicians. He always spoke his mind as to what he believed was the truth, and what was best for his country, regardless of political pressures. He had no tolerance for inefficiency, dishonesty and political gamesmanship. Hence, he was respected by all, from the President of the United States to the laborer in the Canal Zone.

After his military service, Goethals had an opportunity to cash-in on his fame. With the prominence gained from the Canal job, he received many offers that could enrich him if he would lend his name to the ventures. He refused. He remained a humble, consummate public servant.

Due to illness in early 1928, Goethals was prevented from traveling back to the Canal Zone for a celebration and reunion of former workers. Because of his absence, he sent a letter to be read at the celebration. This letter arrived in Panama at the same time that the news of his death arrived by cable. An extract from this letter, summed-up the respect that he had for those under his command: "No leader of any organization ever took greater pride in the spirit of loyalty to the work which animated its entirety, in the cheerful undergoings of hardships when needed, in the overcoming of difficulties that were encountered, and it is real affection which I have for the men who gave willingly to gain the end to which we were striving" (ibid.).

General Goethals' obituary in the New York Times stated that his death "cast a pall of gloom and sorrow over the entire Canal Zone and Panama, where he was loved, admired and respected, as no other man" (ibid.).

....

"Wancantognaka" is a Lakota Indian expression that describes the virtues of individuals who should be in leadership positions. It expresses the central virtues of justice and generosity, and virtues in relationships of giving and receiving (MacIntyre 1999). These are the virtues necessary for leaders who will enable our society to achieve greatness and sustainability. Such leaders are individuals "who recognize responsibilities to immediate family, extended family, and tribe and who express that recognition by their participation in ceremonial acts of uncalculated giving, ceremonies of thanksgiving, of remembrance, and of the conferring of honor. Wancantognaka is the generosity that I owe to all those others who also owe it to me" (ibid.,120).

....

Let's promote leaders with the ability, integrity and justice demonstrated by General Goethals, and with the virtues of Wancantognaka -- our hope for the future!

$\mathfrak{A}$CKNOWLEDGMENTS

I have been a student of governance and corporate ethics throughout my 30-year career as an energy executive. The dearth of ethical leadership in government and business has reached crisis proportions. Over the past four years I gathered information and considered how to present this subject in a substantive, yet palatable way. The King Rat is a synthesis of my observations, wrapped in humor and indignation.

What I observed was how the behavior of greedy, unethical executives parallels that of rats. In 2005, I set out to learn more about the behavioral patterns of rat communities using the excellent resources of the Carnegie Library in Pittsburgh.

Many of my thoughts and ideas were formed by conversations with high caliber business leaders with extraordinary insights into the inner workings of the corporate world.

I would like to thank my wife, children and friend L. Cramer who were most helpful in both the form and substance of the book. The preparation of the manuscript went through several revisions, and for that I thank Denise Wirick.

Finally, I would like to acknowledge the illustrations of Eduardo del Rio, a talented young artist. Eduardo captured the essence of the King Rat and His Court, and hopefully enlivened for readers this most serious of subjects.

WAB

COPYRIGHT PERMISSIONS

Economist

Reproduced with permission of Economist Newspaper Group in the format Tradebook via Copyright Clearance Center.

Copyright	Title
© 2007	Mao and the Art of Management
© 2005	Fat Cats Turn to Low Fat
© 2007	A Special Report on Executive Pay
© 2007	The Making of the Neo-KGB State
© 2002	Survey: Why Honesty is the Best Policy

Forbes

Reprinted by Permission of Forbes Magazine © 2008 Forbes LLC.

Stanford Business

Used with permission of Stanford Business magazine Copyright © 2005. All rights reserved.

Times of London

Used with permission of NI Syndication Ltd. Copyright © 2005. All rights reserved.

USAToday

From USAToday, a division of Gannett Co., Reprinted with Permission.

Copyright	License Number
© 2008	2073641022946

Wall Street Journal

Copyright	License Number	Title
© 2005	2073090174717	Amid Crackdown, the Jet Perk Suddenly Looks a Lot Pricier
© 2006	2073100445850	Interested Parties: In Internal Probes of Stock Options Conflicts Abound
© 2005	2073100732753	As Banks Bid for City Bond Work, 'Pay to Play' Tradition Endures
© 2006	2073101036311	Takeover Artists Quench Thirst
© 2006	2073101424134	Hedge Funds Hire Lobbyists to Gather Tips in Washington
© 2006	2073091477669	Bosses Pay: How Stock Options Became Part of the Problem

Appendix - The DRIAD Test

The **DRIAD** test consists of 50 questions to determine the **Degree of Rat Infestation And Deviance** of your leaders. For each of the questions, score from 1 to 10 the degree that the statement applies to your organization or leader. Remember, it is a matter of degree. Many organizations have some degree of rat infestation and rat-like leaders. The issue about your organization and leadership is whether you are infested to the 2nd or even 1st degree, and whether your leader is a King Rat. Once the questions are answered, add up the total score to determine the **DRIAD** for your organization (see Chapter 22). The minimum "R" ("Rat") score is 0 and the maximum is 500. Each question should be considered independently, reflecting on true observations of your organization's leadership. Some questions have a no (0), maybe (5) or a yes (10) answer; others require you to consider a range of 0 to 10. Answer all of the questions. If you don't know the answer to a question, take a guess based on your intuition and knowledge of related behaviors. The scale below shows the scoring related to your observations:

No						Yes
Never	Rarely	Occasionally	Maybe	Regularly	Usually	Always
0	2	4	5	6	8	10

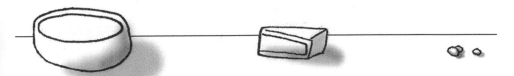

There is no time limit. However, I suspect that you will breeze through the questions, especially if your organization has the misfortune of being led by a King Rat. You may want to write your answers on a separate scoring sheet, so you don't influence others by marking this book.

Score

___ 1. Decisions by the CEO and the board can be linked (directly or circuitously) to payoffs to friends or other persons of influence rather than to maximizing shareholder value.

___ 2. You lie in bed at night wondering how your once excellent organization could have declined to its current state without remedial action by the board.

___ 3. Your organization's senior managers receive unfathomable compensation packages, regardless of performance.

___ 4. Extraordinary efforts are made to shield and protect the CEO and the board from criticism.

___ 5. The CEO and the board show a remarkable lack of interest in the long-term viability of the organization.

___ 6. Company loyalists, leaders with high ethical standards, and managers with demonstrated success are treated with suspicion and are targeted for elimination.

___ 7. Outstanding employees are transferred to positions that are outside the mainstream activities of the company or to remote locations.

___ 8. Organizational changes take place without informing employees and without clear organization charts.

___ 9. Line managers (operations, engineering and sales) are used as scapegoats for poor performance regardless of capability, culpability or prior performance record.

___ 10. The most competent employees leave the organization for other opportunities.

___ 11. New managers and executives are less competent than the individuals they replaced.

___ 12. Meetings with the CEO and the board are restricted to an inner circle of managers so as to not provide exposure to those who are doing the real work of the organization.

___ 13. Those in the CEO's inner circle receive rapid promotions, excessive pay and bonuses, management contracts and responsibilities far beyond their capabilities, while the rest in the organization have benefits cut and pay increases restricted.

___ 14. Inner circle managers have characteristics that make them unsuitable to replace the CEO for a number of years (due to age, personality defects, incompetence, lack of education or inexperience).

___ 15. Inner circle employees sacrifice all moral and ethical considerations in exchange for wealth and power.

___ 16. New board members are nominated by the board's nominating committee under the oversight of the chairman and the CEO based upon past social relationships.

___ 17. Board members are from the "club" of CEOs who are supplementing their income by board membership fees, trading inside information, and enriching their friends in open bi-lateral agreements.

___ 18. Board members serve on many boards and pay little attention to company business; or alternatively, your company is their only board membership (these are usually consultants, lawyers, or local businesspersons) and they depend on the income from your company's board activities to support their lifestyle.

___ 19. Board meetings are away from the headquarters, and the annual meeting is in a remote location to prevent board members from inadvertent exposure to employees and to prevent inadvertent exposure of board members and the CEO to the shareholders.

___ 20. Board members who express independent thoughts or

criticism of the chairman or CEO are given secondary committee assignments and are not nominated to stand for reelection.

___ 21. Consulting agreements, contracts, political contributions, charitable donations, and other payments from corporate funds are made to organizations led by friends of the board members and the CEO.

___ 22. Approved capital projects have connections (although not outwardly apparent) to friends or relatives of board members, the CEO or politicos.

___ 23. Management consultants and executive search firms are hired (regardless of need) in order to deflect responsibility for personnel decisions and to endear the CEO to the firms for future job recommendations.

___ 24. After the competent employees have been removed, lucrative consulting assignments, even in areas of core-competencies, are given to friends of the board members and the CEO.

___ 25. The board provides lavish compensation, golden parachutes, management contracts and stock options to the CEO regardless of performance, in exchange for renomination and increased compensation.

___ 26. The CEO rarely comes out of his office and has his own personal entrance, bathroom and parking space to avoid employees. The CEO only meets with employees in highly structured and choreographed events.

___ 27. The CEO "speaks" though the members of his inner circle, and especially through the head of public relations. The exception to this rule is when there is good news to report (which is seldom).

___ 28. The CEO has company-paid luxurious, jet aircraft used for corporate and personal trips for himself, his friends, consultants, politicos and board members. The aircraft is used for entertaining, usually at sporting events, and for hunting and fishing trips. At the same time, the working aircraft for operations, engineering, and sales managers (who have legitimate needs) are eliminated for "cost savings."

___ 29. The CEO and his inner circle never let their schedules or locations be known, so that the presumption is they are actually working; whereas, the opposite is typically the case. The cell phone, Blackberry and fax machine enable this stealth behavior.

___ 30. The CEO never puts anything in writing or email, so as to prevent leaving a paper or electronic trail; at the same time he establishes a surveillance system to monitor employee communications and activities.

___ 31. Bad news is covered up with propaganda in press releases from the public and investor relations departments.

___ 32. Good news is always presented by the CEO to the public and to the investment community, or, if presented by press release, the CEO is quoted and glorified (quotes written by ghost writers).

___ 33. Poor financial performance is always reported by the CFO and attributed to events beyond the control of management.

___ 34. Operators, engineers and sales executives are regularly sacrificed whenever pressure begins to build on the CEO.

___ 35. Consultants, investment bankers and other mercenaries are used frequently by the CEO and the board to buy protection.

___ 36. The CEO spends an inordinate amount of time dwelling on how to manipulate the stock price rather than focusing on the underlying business.

___ 37. Private meetings with mutual, hedge and private equity fund managers are high on the priority list of the CEO.

___ 38. The CEO has extraordinary concern for influencing the short-term stock price (up or down) rather than with the long-term value of the business.

___ 39. Investment houses that provide good ratings by their analysts for your company's stock amazingly are the successful bidders for investment banking business. Conversely, poor ratings result in curtailed access to the CEO and no banking business.

___ 40. The CEO is given special trading privileges unavailable to the average person due to his relationship with the investment banking, mutual fund and hedge fund managers.

___ 41. Financial support to politicos from personal donations and corporate donations, honoraria, boondoggles to exotic locations, and the use of "go-to consultants" for political payoffs are acceptable behaviors in your company.

___ 42. Hiring of the relatives of judges, legislators and regulators is considered to be good business practice, regardless of qualifications.

___ 43. The highest priced legal talent available is retained by the organization to protect and defend the CEO and the board members.

___ 44. The highest priority of the CEO and the board of directors is to ensure that they have exceptional directors' and officers' insurance.

___ 45. Extraordinary time and expense are committed to legal and financial advisors to ensure that the CEO and the board meet the form (but not the substance) of laws and regulations.

___ 46. Company newspapers, external publications and annual reports lavish extraordinary praise on the CEO.

___ 47. The company's public relations effort heavily publicizes the awards and recognition received from organizations and publications, albeit such awards and recognition may have been in exchange for purchasing goods or services from the organization or by placing ads in the publications.

___ 48. The public relations department not only reports the strategy of the company, but also creates a Potemkin village and then puts the words into the CEO's mouth.

___ 49. Half-truths are the norm rather than the exception in PR releases.

___ 50. Corporate publications become glossy, filled with color and adorned with pictures of the CEO and members of his inner circle. No expense is spared to glorify the CEO.

Total R score

Find out the degree of rat infestation in your organization and deviance of your CEO by comparing the total R score with the ranges shown in Chapter 22.

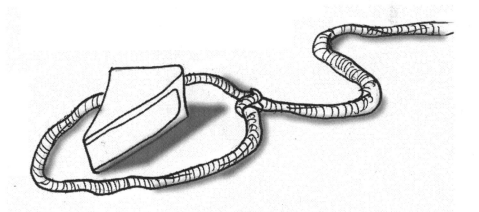

SOURCES FOR SECTION/CHAPTER QUOTATIONS

Section	**I**	Wells 1964, 34.
Chapter	**1**	Clavell 1962, 490.
	2	Ferris and Griffith 1949, 2.
	3	Bekoff 2004, 712.
	4	Whishaw and Gorney 1991, 190.
	5	Bermant 1973, 280.
	6	Skinner 1938, 38.
	7	Whishaw and Gorney 1991, 185.
Section	**II**	Faulkner 1962, 121.
Chapter	**8**	Zimmer 2000, 168-169.
	9	Bekoff 2004, 363-364.
	10	Grzimek 2003, 75-76.
	11	Morris and Beer 2003, 84.
	12	Mizner 2006.
	13	Thornton and Zegel 2005, 35.
	14	Khurana 2002, 205 and 211.
	15	Barnett 1963, 61.
	16	Sullivan 2004, 97.
	17	Morris and Beer 2003, 98-99.
Section	**III**	Jackman 1984, 77
Chapter	**18**	Brown 1959, 22-23.
	19	Burton 1978, 62.
Section	**IV**	Jackman 1984, 76.
Chapter	**20**	Atkinson 2004, 498.
	21	Flanagan 2003, 11.
	22	Dylan 2006.
Section	**V**	Curnult 2001, 490.
Chapter	**23**	Ehrlich 1998, 143.
	24	Browning 2003,147.
	25	Bishop and Bishop 1930, 467.

SOURCES FOR SIDEBAR QUOTATIONS

Page	Publication	Author	Date	Source Page
9	*Wall Street Journal*	Maramont, Mark	May 25, 2005	A1
13	*Economist*		Dec 22, 2007	123-124
23	*Economist*		Mar 5, 2005	14
25	*New Yorker*	Surowrecki, James	Jan 22, 2007	32
31	*Boston Globe*		May 2, 2005	
33	*Wall Street Journal*	Maremont and Forelle	Dec 27, 2006	A1
37	*Economist*		Jan 20, 2007	4
43	*Stanford Business*	Barrett, Todd	Feb 2005	32
51	*Business Week*	France and Carney	Jul 1, 2002	
59	*PR News*		Feb 9, 2004	1
61	*Across the Board*	Budd, John	May 1, 2003	11
65	*Economist*		Aug 25, 2007	26
81	*Economist*		Mar 9, 2002	9

Page	Publication	Author	Date	Source Page
87	*Wall Street Journal*	Bandler and Forelle	Aug 11, 2006	A1
89	*Wall Street Journal*	Whitehouse, Mark	Mar 25, 2005	A1
101	*Times of London*	Irving, Richard	Nov 14, 2005	48
103	*USA Today*	Jones and Iwata	Sept 29, 2008	B4
113	*International Herald Tribune*		Apr 16, 2008	
115	*Forbes.com*	Fisher, Daniel	Oct 16, 2006	
119	*Wall Street Journal*	Sender, Henry	Jan 5, 2006	C1
133	*Accounting Today*	Klein, Melissa	Jul 22, 2002	1
141	*Wall Street Journal*	Mullins and Scannell	Dec 8, 2006	A1
145	*Nation*	Greider, William	Feb 4, 2002	11

BIBLIOGRAPHY

Aguilar, Francis J. 1994. Managing corporate ethics: Learning from America's ethical companies how to supercharge business performance. New York: Oxford University Press.

Allen, Jeff and Duane Davis. 1993. Assessing some determinant effects of ethical consulting behavior: The case of personal and professional values. Journal of Business Ethics: 12:6:449-459.

Atkinson, Rob. 2004. Connecting business ethics and legal ethics for the common good: Come let us reason together. The Journal of Corporation Law: Spring: vol 29:issue 3:470-531.

Bandler, James and Charles Forelle. 2006. Interested Parties: In Internal Probes of Stock Options Conflicts Abound. Wall Street Journal: Aug 11:A1.

Barash, David P. 2004. Caught between choices: Personal gain vs. public good. Chronicle of Higher Education: April 16:vol 50:issue 32:B13-14.

Barnett, S.A. 1963. The rat: A study in behavior. Chicago: Aldine Publishing Company.

Barrett, Todd. 2005. Read the fine print: We dare you. Stanford Business: Feb:32.

Baum, Herb. 2004. The transparent leader: How to build a great company through straight talk, openness and accountability. New York: Harper Business.

Bekoff, Marc, ed. 2004. Encyclopedia of animal behavior. Westport CT: Greenwood Press.

Bella, David A., Jonathan B. King and David Kailin. 2003. The dark side of organizations and a method to reveal it. Emergence: 5:3:66-82.

Bermant, Gordon, ed. 1973. Perspectives on animal behavior, a first course. Ten original essays by John Alcock (and others). Essay by Robert C. Bolles, The comparative psychology of learning: The selective association principle and some problems with the "general" laws of learning. Glenview, IL: Scott, Foresman and Company.

Bertrand, Marsha. 2000. Fraud! How to protect yourself from schemes, scams, and swindles. New York: AMACOM.

Bishop, Joseph Bucklin and Franham Bishop. 1930. Goethals, Genius of the Panama Canal. New York: Harper & Brothers.

Black, Dawn. 1996. Many executives are tempted to commit fraud study asserts. Wall Street Journal: March 26: C1 and C15.

Boot, Kelvin. 1985. The nocturnal naturalist. Newton Abbot, Devon; North Pamfret, VT: David & Charles.

Boston Globe. 2005. Bad Image for Polaroid. May 2.

Brown, John Russell ed. 1959. The Merchant of Venice: The Arden edition of the works of William Shakespeare. Cambridge, MA: Harvard University Press.

Browning, Robert. 2003. The pied piper of hamelin. in Poetry X Jun 16:http://poetry.poetryx.com/poems/147.

Bruner, Robert F. and Lynn Sharp Paine. 1988. Management buyouts and managerial ethics. California Management Review: Winter:30:2:89-107.

Bruno, Anna. 2005. William James. E-mail communication: March 16.

Budd, John F, Jr. 2003. Where were the PR wizards? Across the Board. May 1:11.

Buffett, Warren. 2006. Letter to Shareholders. Berkshire Hathaway 2005 Annual Report: Feb 28:17.

Burrell, Gibson. 1988. Modernism, post modernism and organizational analysis: The contribution of Michel Foucault. Organizational Studies: vol 9:issue 2:221-236.

Burton Maurice. 1978. Just like an animal. New York: Charles Scribner's Sons.

Cannon, John, and Ralph Griffiths. 1988. The Oxford illustrated history of the British monarchy. New York: Oxford University Press.

Clavell, James. 1962. King rat. New York: Delta Publishing.

Cohen, William A. and Nurit Cohen. 1993. The paranoid corporation and 8 other ways your company can be crazy. New York: AMACOM.

Collins, James C. 2001. Good to great: Why some companies make the leap...and others don't. New York: Harper Business.

Compensation and Benefits for Law Offices. 2004. Rainmaking: What all your junior lawyers need to know and do. August: 4:8:5-10.

Curnult, Jordan. 2001. Animals and the law: A source book. Santa Barbara, CA: ABC-CLIO.

Dalai Lama. 1999. Ethics for the new millennium: His Holiness the Dalai Lama. New York: Riverhead Books.

Davia, Howard R. 2000. Fraud 101:Techniques and strategies for detection. New York: John Wiley & Sons, Inc.

Dobson, John. 2003. Why ethics codes don't work. Financial Analysts Journal: Nov/Dec 59:6:29-34.

Dugatkin, Lee Alan. 2000. The imitation factor: Evolution beyond the gene. New York: The Free Press.

Dylan, Bob. 2006. Subterranean Homesick Blues. http://bobdylan.com/songs/subterranean.html.

Economist. 2002a. Survey: Why honesty is the best policy. Mar 9:9.

Economist. 2002b. Bosses for sale. Oct 5:57-58.

Economist. 2003. Perils in the saving pool: Scandal is tainting one of the most successful forms of saving ever invented. Nov 8:65-67.

Economist. 2005a. The new money men. Feb 19:63-66.

Economist. 2005b. Business schools: Bad for business? Feb 19:57-58.

Economist. 2005c. Fat cats turn to low fat. March 5:14.

Economist. 2006. The paranoid style in American politics. Jan 7:32.

Economist. 2007a. A special report on executive pay. Jan 20:1-20.

Economist. 2007b. The making of the neo-KGB state. Aug 25:25-28.

Economist. 2007c. Mao and the art of management. Dec 22:123-124.

Ehrlich, Henry, Comp. 1998. The Wiley book of business quotations. New York: John Wiley & Sons Inc.

Faulkner, William. 1962. The reivers: A reminiscence. New York: Random House.

Ferris, Edmond J. and John Q. Griffith, Jr., ed. 1949. The rat in laboratory investigation. New York: Hafner Publishing Company.

Fisher, Daniel. 2006. A dangerous game. Forbes.com:Oct16. http://forbes.com/forbes/2006/1016/040_print.html.

Flanagan, William G. 2003. Dirty rotten CEOs: How business

leaders are fleecing America. New York: Citadel Press.

France, Mike and Dan Carney. 2002. Why Corporate Crooks are tough to nail. Business Week. July 1.

Galbraith, John Kenneth. 2004. The economics of innocent fraud: Truth for our time. Boston: Houghton Mifflin.

Gil-White, Francisco J. and Joe Henrich. 2000. The evaluation of prestige. Working Papers, Faculty – University of Michigan Business School: 1-107.

Gilbreath, Alice. 1979. Creatures of the night: Nocturnal animals of North America. New York: David McKay Company, Inc.

Grant, Colin. 2004. The altruist's dilemma. Business Ethics Quarterly: April:14:315.

Greider, William. 2002. Crime in the suites. The Nation. Feb 4:11.

Grzimek, Bernhard. 2003. Grzimek's animal life encyclopedia. 2nd Ed. Vol. 2 Detroit: Gale.

Hanson, David P. 1991. Managing for ethics: Some implications of research on the prisoners' dilemma game. SAM Advanced Management Journal: 56:16-21.

Harrington, Alan. 1959. Life in the crystal palace. New York: Knopf.

Hendrickson, Robert. 1983. More cunning than man: A social

history of rats and men. New York: Stein and Day.

Hill, Ivan, ed. 1976. The ethical basis of economic freedom. Essay by Ivan Hill, The meaning of ethics and freedom. Chapel Hill, NC: American Viewpoint Inc.

Hoffman, Charles. 1971. The Maoist economic model. Journal of Economic Issues: Sept:vol 5:issue 3:12-28.

Huxley, Aldous. 1958. Brave new world revisited. New York: Harper.

International Herald Tribune. 2008. Top hedge fund managers collect windfall fees in 2007. Apr 16:http://iht.com/articles/ap/2008/04/16/business/NA-FIN-US-Hedge-Funds.php.

Irving, Richard. 2005. Price to pay for knowing too much. Times of London: Nov 14:48.

Jackman, Michael, Edited. 1984. The Macmillan book of business and economic quotations. New York: MacMillan Publishing Company.

Johnson, Elmer W. 1990. Ethics and corporate governance in the age of pension fund capitalism. From the Andrew R. Cecil lectures on moral values in a free society established by the University of Texas. Artzt, Edwin L., et al. Our Economic System: Its Strength and Weaknesses. Austin, TX: The University of Texas Press.

Johnson, Spencer. 1998. Who moved my cheese? New York: G.P. Putnum's Sons.

Jones, Del and Edward Iwata. 2008. CEO pay takes a hit in bailout plan. USA Today:Sept 29.

Kets de Vries, Manfred, F.R. and Danny Miller. 1987. Unstable at the top: Inside the troubled organization. New York: The New American Library.

Keyes, Ralph. 2004. The post-truth era: Dishonesty and deception in contemporary life. New York: St. Martin's Press.

Khurana, Rakesh. 2002. Searching for a corporate savior: The irrational quest for charismatic CEOs. Princeton, NJ: Princeton University Press.

Kihn, Martin. 2005. House of lies: How management consultants steal your watch and then tell you the time. New York: Warner Business Books.

Klein, Melissa. 2002. Academia: Audit committees may be key to restoring confidence. Accounting Today:July 22:1.

Laaksonen, Oiva. 1984. The management and power structure of Chinese enterprises during and after the cultural revolution with empirical data comparing Chinese and European enterprises. Organization Studies: 5:1-27.

Lane III, Frederick S. 2003. The naked employee: How technology is compromising workplace privacy. New York: AMACOM.

MacIntyre, Alasdair C. 1999. Dependent rational animals: Why human beings need the virtues. Chicago, IL: Open Court.

Maremont, Mark. 2005. Amid crackdown, the jet perk suddenly looks a lot pricier. Wall Street Journal: May 25:A1 and A8.

Maremont, Mark and Charles Forelle.2006. Bosses' Pay: How Stock Options Became Part of the Problem. Wall Street Journal:Dec 27:A1 and A6.

Mechling, Thomas B. 1974. The mythical ethics of law, pr, and accounting. Business and Society Review: Winter 76/77:20:6-10.

Michels, Robert. 1962. Political parties: A sociological study of the oligarchical tendencies of modern democracy. Translated by Eden and Cedar Paul. New York: Free Press.

Milgram, Stanley. 1974. Obedience to authority. New York: Harper & Row.

Mill, John Stuart. 1874. A system of logic. Eighth Edition. New York: Harper & Brothers.

Mizner, Wilson. 2006. Wilson Mizner quotes. http://en.thinkexist. com/quotations.

Moore, Adam D. 2000. Employee monitoring and computer technology: Evaluative surveillance vs. privacy. Business Ethics Quarterly:10:697.

Morris, Pat and Amy-Jane Beer. 2003. World of animals, Vol. 7,

Mammals. Danbury CT: Grolier.

Mullins, Brody and Kara Scannell.2006. Hedge funds hire lobbyists to gather tips in Washington. Wall Street Journal: Dec 8:A1 and A15.

New York Times. 1928. Gen. Goethals dies after long illness. Jan 22.

Orwell, George. 1954. Animal Farm. New York: Harcourt Brace & Company.

Orwell, George. 1949. 1984. New York: Harcourt Brace & Company.

PR News. 2004. Make room on PR plate to enhance business ethics. Feb 9:1.

Persky, Joseph. 1995. The ethology of homo economicus. Journal of Economic Perspectives: Spring:9:2:221-231.

Press, Bill. 2001. Spin this!: All the ways we don't tell the truth. New York: Pocket Books.

Rampton, Sheldon and John Stauber. 2001. Trust us, We're the experts: How industry manipulates science and gambles with your future. New York: Jeremy P. Tarcher/ Putnum.

Rasiel, Ethan M. 1999. The McKinsey way: Using the techniques of the world's top strategic consultants to help you and your business. New York: McGraw-Hill.

Reardon, Kathleen Kelley. 2001. The secret handshake: Mastering the politics of the business inner circle. New York: Currency/ Doubleday.

Regalado, Antonio. 2005. Ethics of U.S. scientists may be shaky, poll says. Wall Street Journal: June 9:D4.

Rombauer, Irma S. and Marion Rombauer Becker. 1975. The joy of cooking. Indianapolis, IN: Bobs-Merrill Co.

Rosenbaum, Thane. 2004. The myth of moral justice: Why our legal system fails to do what's right. New York: Harper Collins.

Sender, Henry. 2006. Takeover artists quench thirst. Wall Street Journal: Jan 5:C1 and C4.

Skinner, B.F. 1938. The behavior of organisms: An experimental analysis. Englewood Cliffs, NJ: Prentice-Hall Inc.

Solomon, Deborah and Anne Marie Squeo. 2005. Crackdown puts corporations, executives in new legal peril. Wall Street Journal: June 20:A1.

Southwick, Charles H. 1970. Animal aggression: Selected readings. New York: Van Nostrand Reinhold Company.

Stanford Business. 2005. Irrationality can pay dividends. Feb:26-27.

Stevens, Mark. 1987. The insiders: The truth behind the scandal rocking Wall Street. New York: G.P. Putnum's Sons.

Stewart, James B. 1991. Den of thieves. New York: Simon & Shuster.

Sullivan, Robert. 2004. Rats: Observations on the history & habitat of the city's most unwanted inhabitants. New York: Bloomsbury.

Surowiecki, James. 2007. The Sky High Club. The New Yorker: Jan 22:32

Tam, Pui-Wing, Erin White, Nick Wingfield and Kris Maher. 2005. Snooping e-mail by software is now a workplace norm. Wall Street Journal-Eastern Edition: March 9: B1-B3.

Thornton, Emily and Susan Zegel. 2005. Hedge funds: The new raiders. Business Week: Feb 28:32-35.

Toffler, Alvin. 1990. Power shift: Knowledge, wealth and violence at the edge of the 21st century. New York: Bantam Books.

Tullock, Gordon. 1985. Adam Smith and the prisoners' dilemma. Quarterly Journal of Economics: 100:4:1073-1081.

Van Es, Robert. 2002. Impartial advocates to political agents: Role switching and trustworthiness in consulting. Journal of Business Ethics: 39:145-152.

Vandekerckhove, Wm and M.S. Ronald Commons. 2003. Downward workplace mobbing: A sign of the times. Journal of Business Ethics: 45:41-51.

Vickers, Marcia, Mike France, Emily Thorton, David Henry, Heather Timmons and Mike McNamee. 2002. How corrupt is Wall Street? Business Week: May 13:36-42.

Wells, T.A.G. 1964. The rat: A practical guide. London: Heinemann Educational Books.

Whishaw, Ian Q., and Boguslaw P. Gorney. 1991. The defensive strategies of foraging rats: A review and synthesis. Psychological Record: Spring:41:2:185-205.

Whitehouse, Mark. 2005. As banks bid for city bond work, 'Pay to play' tradition endures. Wall Street Journal: March 25:A1.

Yermack, David. 2005a. Flights of fancy: Corporate jets, CEO perquisites, and inferior shareholder returns. March. AFA 2005 Philadelphia Meetings. http://ssm.com/abstract.

Yermack, David. 2005b. Golden handshakes: Separation pay for retired and dismissed CEOs. November. http://ssm.com/abstract.

Zimbardo, Phillip. 2006. Stanford prison experiment. http://prisonexp.org.

Zimmer, Carl. 2000. Parasite rex: Inside the bizarre world of nature's most dangerous creatures. New York: The Free Press.

ABOUT THE ILLUSTRATOR

Eduardo Paul del Rio was born in Salamanca, Spain and grew up on the fiercely tilled farmlands of Yuba City, in Northern California. He received his Bachelor's degree in Spanish Literature from the University of San Francisco and studied illustration at the Universidad de Salamanca.

del Rio has spent the last several years working as a commercial and fine artist in San Francisco. His oil paintings and sculptures have been featured in galleries throughout the San Francisco area, and he has directed creative projects for many top global brands.

Today, del Rio lives and works in New York City. In his work, the densely layered urban spaces of New York are intertwined with the imagery and grace of an older world and the limitless innovative spirit of California. Perhaps del Rio's heart resides in California and his soul resides in Spain. Evocatively, his passion transcends place and time.

Select work can be viewed at www.PencilProne.com.

ABOUT THE AUTHOR

William (Bill) Bruno worked in corporate offices boardrooms of major corporations for over 30 years. His pri interests are corporate governance, leadership ethics, internat energy security and sustainable development. He has bee international speaker in energy forums and a lecturer to class the Department of Defense and Department of Energy.

A native of Greenwich, Connecticut, he received Bach of Science with distinction and Masters of Engineering degree civil engineering from Cornell University. At Cornell, he tailo his studies into an interdisciplinary program of earth scienc sociology, economics and environmental law--which today wou be known as the study of sustainable development. At the Gradua School of Business at Stanford University, he received a Masters Business Administration. Bruno joined the energy industry durin the height of the first energy crisis, and embarked on a career a an energy executive.

In addition to his accomplishments in the energy industry, Bruno served as a Captain in the United States Army Corps of Engineers, is a registered civil engineer in the State of New York, a Member of the American Society of Civil Engineers, a consultant to energy companies and Wall Street equity investors, and has served as an officer and board member for nonprofit institutions including a community hospital in Pittsburgh where he organized and chaired a new committee to champion improvements in clinical quality and patient safety.

Bill and his wife, Lynne, are the parents of two children -- William James Bruno and Anna Lynne Bruno. Bill and Lynne reside in Pittsburgh, Pennsylvania and Vineyard Haven, Massachusetts.

Made in the USA
Charleston, SC
15 December 2010